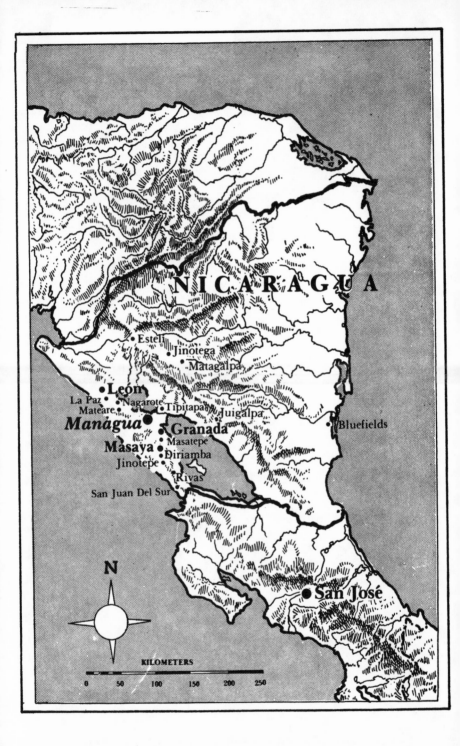

N I C A R A G U A

Estelí
Jinotega
Matagalpa
León
La Paz
Mateare Nagarote Tipitapa Juigalpa
Managua Granada Bluefields
Masaya Masatepe
Diriamba
Jinotepe Rivas
San Juan Del Sur

San José

N

KILOMETERS

0   50   100   150   200   250

Cocktails at Somoza's

by Richard Elman

A Reporter's Sketchbook of Events in Revolutionary Nicaragua

Apple-wood Books   1982   Cambridge/Watertown

The following stories were printed in nearly identical versions in magazines: "An Incident in León" and "Irwin" in *The Iowa Review*; "Tipitapa Baths" in #; "La Paz Centro" in *The Nation*; and "Managua's Only French Restaurant" in *Houston City Magazine*. The poem "Leaving Nicaragua" also appeared in Richard Elman's collection *In Chontales* (Street Press). A section of "Revolution" originally appeared in *Geo*.

Copyright © 1981, 1982 Richard Elman

ISBN: 0-918222-43-5

All rights reserved. Printed in the United States of America. No part of this book may be used or reproduced in any manner whatsoever without written permission, except in the case of brief quotations embodied in critical articles and reviews. For information write to Apple-wood Books, Inc., Box 2870, Cambridge, Massachusetts 02139.

Cocktails
at
Somoza's

for my co-workers and colleagues

Susan Meiselas
Matt Naythons
Alma Guillermoprieto
Mark Starr
Alan Riding, and others;
and for MCJ, and the staff of **La Prensa**,
Manuel of Monimbo, and "Armando"—
to a girl hitchhiking along
a road; thanks, congratulations . . .
& to loving Alice,
and her various arts,
and in memory of those who fell: presente!

This is a work of fact, of
Time as I remember it through
the people I was with, and
the truth of any story, in this
case, I would hope, as in all
others, is with the showing, and
the telling.

My Spanish is imperfect; I've
translated all speech and writing
unless I felt specific words and
phrases were so familiar they
could remain in argot. I have
changed names and identities, without inventing
anything, so that certain persons
important to these stories would
not feel compromised.

Richard Elman
Hotel Maria Cristina
Mexico City

Contents

"Every Nicaraguan is a Sandinistan combatant, a guerrilla, a sniper, a struggler, a resistant, a raiser of barricades..."
—**Translation from a rebel broadcast made over Radio Mundial, September 6, 1978, when the then Somoza-controlled station was occupied briefly by Sandinistan forces.**

"God may like a Dictator who hails from Nicaragua, but He doesn't want him to be the *dictator of Nicaragua..."*
—**Trappist padre Ernesto Cardenal, "To Live Is To Love,"** *Meditations on Love & Spirituality*, **Doubleday Image Books.**

"Masaya, totally free! so many fell there..."
—**Ernesto Cardenal, "Lights"**

Overheard conversation between a young Sandinistan and his comandante in the lobby of The Intercontinental Hotel, Managua, after the victory:
"Nicaragua no es en el hotel. Nicaragua es afuera."
("Nicaragua is not in this hotel. Nicaragua is outside this.")

This letter was received from a Nicaraguan friend six weeks after the Sandinistan victory over the Somozas.

September 10, 1979

Dear Richard:

Today I received, at the same time, your four letters ...Here we now lack a post office, because the entire center of our city remains a ruin, after the genocidal bombings of Somoza.

I am giving this letter to my wife to be mailed in Managua today where she is going to celebrate mass on the anniversary of the death of her brother, my in-law, killed by the National Guard in the capital a year ago.

Nicaragua has been left bankrupt; the war's end mixes confusion with contradiction. I served in the Sandinistan army during the battle, in the romantically named "Ultimate Brigade," and I suffered lacerations in the right leg from the explosion of an incendiary bomb, from which I have only now recovered. Even so, the day we finally took the city and Somoza fled, I asked to be relieved of my duties and turned in my weapon...

As you know, this country remains totally destroyed, in ruins; as the peasants say, "with these oxen one must plow."

It makes me happy to learn you are enjoying the primitive pleasures of matrimony. Our house suffered so much destruction during the war and now remains almost entirely wrecked within, the consequence of machine gunning and the bombing by airplanes, and so we have taken ourselves, with all we could salvage, a little further down the block to my mother's house. Here we shall stay until the house can be repaired, which should take some time.

The arrival of liberty is a satisfaction that one now takes in like the air one breathes, like life itself, its joy. All the privations and sufferings of previous years shall have to be obliterated. When we were alone, when we felt exiled and sad and in despair, without any more strength to support our dignity, friendships such as yours, with your fraternal solidarity, reaffirmed our courage.

I shall remember you always. Now all must work for the revolution without much profit at present and still at a great sacrifice ("when the war ends/the revolution marches forward"); later, when we have recuperated from the destruction and rebuilt our economy, we shall invite you to come to Nicaragua. It's a country on the march. I spend my days now like the Indians here and, at night, read a little. I'm still not able to bring myself to write about this. It will require a new vocabulary; war is sad. I embrace you.

I

A Returning Glance

Returning

Early on a gray, cloudy, muggy Friday morning in September, 1979 I finally got back to Managua, a year after I had left the town in the middle of its revolution. The only other plane on the runway of the August Sandino airport this time was a Soviet Aeroflot jet which had just brought over President Pham Van Dong of Vietnam from a conference of the nonaligned nations in Cuba to celebrate Nicaragua's Independence Day with the victorious Sandinistan cadres and their supporters.

The airport lounge and customs area looked like a Sandinistan rally: so many intense-looking young boys and girls in captured National Guard uniforms. Their *rojonegro* scarves, bandanas, pins, and badges were their only insignia. They all carried weapons liberated from the Somocista military: long Israeli *galil* assault rifles, squat Uzi machine pistols, and American M-16s. Only a few of them had the costly Belgian FN assault rifles that the Revolution had had to purchase on the open market to arm its supporters. Nobody toted shotguns and .22s anymore, such as I remembered from earlier days. Many of the militants were in their early 20s or younger, some much younger: the skinny boy with acne who went through my bags at customs could not have been more than sixteen.

So many weapons everywhere frightened me. Their dangling menace put me off. Bristling with armaments, the young went about their duties as if they were not encumbrances but practical aids to whatever work they were doing. There had to be, I felt, a certain licit hostility intended when those at whom the weapons were once aimed were now swaggering about armed with these same weapons, seemingly always prepared to point them now at others like myself.

Such young people always seemed to be in a state of alert. The wrong word spoken or gesture made could lead to gunfire I believed, but I experienced no lack of revolutionary courtesies from those who were armed or the couple of customs men in civilian clothes whom I recognized from Somoza's time. A woman was helped with her bulky possessions and thanks were accepted.

A Sandinistan comandante asked us to form two ranks, one for Nicaraguans and one for foreigners. He was dark and very sleek and good-looking. He toted a .45 in a thonged leather holster, and then we waited to go before some more of the troops with our open valises.

Security was pretty strict. Despite the advertising displays for the late Howard Hughes's Hotel Intercontinental, The Nicaraguan Coffee Institute, and other apparent holdovers from the anonymous societies of the previous regime, the airport lounge seemed shabby and dingy, like one of those stores that holds a going-out-of-business sale every day in the week. Our small party of arrivals from San José, Costa Rica included some Americans, East and West Germans, Spanish, Japanese, Bulgarians, Peruvians, Canadians, and Ecuadorians. I could perceive no differences in the treatment accorded to any of these nationalities.

There was also the usual complement of returning Nicaraguans: a businessman from Managua who'd lost everything in the bombing and subsequent looting of his office-supplies store; a pharmacist bombed-out from Matagalpa; a paterfamilias of part Jewish extraction who was retired and lived with his children in San Juan, Puerto

Rico and hadn't been home to Nicaragua for twenty-five years; and a couple of university students whom I had first spotted in San José reading copies of the fine leftist Mexican newspaper, *Uno Mas Uno*.

The Sandinistan customs guards were looking for arms and other such contraband, like military radios or equipment of any sort that could be used by counter-revolutionaries. The skinny sixteen-year-old I spoke of earlier also confiscated a copy of *Playboy* from an American female traveler ahead of me, loudly declared it to be "imperialist pornography," tore it into as many pieces as there were people on the line, and threw all these little pieces into a nearby trash container.

Not liking destruction of any written words by anybody, I was as offended as I was surprised. But the woman kept her cool. She was bringing in the *Playboy* and other such magazines for herself and her Borden Company executive husband (who had never left Nicaragua during the fighting), and she was allowed to take through customs copies of such imperialist propaganda 'stroke' sheets as *Better Homes & Gardens, Redbook,* and *Ladies Home Journal*. Moreover, when one visiting journalist had his olive-green military fatigues confiscated, he was assured by a couple of Sandinistans that he would be able to retrieve them once more on leaving Nicaragua.

Still, ripping up *Playboy* did bother me a lot as I waited on line. Dammit all, you just don't destroy the printed word. Even bad writing should not be destroyed. It isn't nice to do that. Never mind the tits and ass in *Playboy*, there are occasionally words I like to read in the magazine; and I thought of an interview I'd found recently with Marlon Brando. And *Playboy*, unlike most American consumer magazines, had at least considered the possibility of sending me back to Nicaragua during the fighting. The plain fact was that most of the U.S. commercial press, with notable exceptions, was so embarrassed by revolutionary events in Nicaragua that they gave them as little coverage as they could. I couldn't even get my letters, which asked for relief for the Nicaraguan people and nonrecognition of the Somozas, published in *New York Review of Books* or the *New York Times*.

But *Playboy* had, at least, considered me for an assignment to Nicaragua, though things were moving too fast by then for their deadlines, they said; and besides, as many New York editors like to say, Central America just doesn't sell *bubkas* in print or even pictures. Moreover, there is a considerable body of U.S editorial ignorance about Central American politics. I can remember one otherwise sophisticated New York publisher, when I asked for a set of press credentials so I would not have to fear intimidation from Somocista officialdom, declaring to me: "Sure I will give them to you, but I just don't know how that's gonna help you with those Sandinistan terrorists down there."

Now, after the Sandinista victory, on this my second trip to Nicaragua, I was paying my own way, because I wanted to see some of the changes the revolution was bringing about, and I wanted to embrace old friends.

So I had borrowed some travel money, and made the only plans I could: to fly to Managua via Mexico City, and San José via the Mormon-owned airline, TACA, since all the other interconnecting stateside flights to Managua were booked solid with returning exiles. Unfortunately, this was the hurricane season in the Caribbean so I was delayed one extra day in Mexico City by storms, and then two days more in San José, Costa Rica.

I've always liked the bustle and hustle and general civil peace of this small, busy, park-filled city compared to a city at war, though this time, as I walked the streets of Costa Rica's metropolis, I was aware of a shabby fringe on all the decencies of prosperity: the elegant shops and the drabness of so many people, dingily dressed, with broken scuffed shoes; of that large pristine marble-columned private club in the center of town which I was barred from entering by a guard, and the open-air sweat shops of the barrios where women sewed blouses and skirts for export. The ads for retirement villages for U.S. pensioners and the cynicism of the English-language *Tico Times* (a kind of sneer) and all the U.S. products such as Tampax and Tech Hi-Fi and Thom McAn desert boots (in a leather-producing country) seemed to testify to the fact that Costa Rica (and probably for its own good) had stuck its head a little above the poverty and medievalisms of Central America to become a fully-integrated member of the U.S. Empire.

But you could buy the Trappist poet Ernesto Cardenal's Nicaraguan poetry anthology in any one of the many nice San José bookstores, whereas the only bookstore I knew of in Nicaragua, at present, was in Masaya, and didn't have too much left on its shelves except revolutionary pamphlets. And during the war you could even talk to Ernesto Cardenal in a mansion in San José, where he was given refuge, he and all the other revolutionists against Somoza. So why knock a rock just because it's small and solid? These two countries had different histories and destinies. In rejecting the U.S.-supported Somoza dynasty, I knew, Nicaragua was, in part, rejecting the sort of dim possibilities that had allowed Costa Rica to prosper a little. The Nicaraguans had been aided in that by many Costa Ricans, including former President Figueres (who confessed in the press to hand-loading planes with arms for the Sandinistans in Nicaragua), because Costa Ricans did sympathize, in the main, with the struggle in their long-oppressed neighboring state. There was also a colony of about 30,000 exiled Chileans in Costa Rica who really knew what it was like to lose a revolution.

A San José friend had told me once, "We are much better off here than in Nicaragua, even though the energy situation is hard on a tiny agricultural country such as this, but all that is only for the moment. Who knows what it may be like with us and them ten years from now? They will surely show us plenty..."

The envy was only hinted at, but there was also pride in his voice that his neighbors had overthrown an oligarchy's tyranny.

Everywhere I went I experienced that pride from Latin

Americans of all sorts, including some exiled Cubans.

I also experienced vestiges of the Empire in action. In a bar in San José I met an American rancher who raised, slaughtered, froze, and marketed "portion-controlled" steaks to the Japanese at forty dollars per steak. A cargo plane arrived every week from the Far East to pick up a load in Panama so prosperous Japanese businessmen could have their rare six-ounce beef steaks aplenty. His financing on the project came from Panama, source of much risk capital these days and a tax haven. He kept saying, "Some people are getting so rich in Panama."

"They sold arms to the Sandinistans," he told me, "and they laundered Somoza's money, too. Panama is the tail wagging the dog of our Empire, I tell you. Tail wagging dog until it hurts..."

There was the ex-Rumanian Iron Guardsman from Baton Rouge who built CIA installations in Colombia; and the guy from Compton, California who claimed he wanted to sell the Sandinistans a division's worth of U.S. arms wholesale in return for a chain of dry-cleaning stores; and the squat little Cuban exile, employee of a multinational company, who thought the Communists would take over Nicaragua and give it to the Cubans unless his company was able to get the labor terms it desired from the Sandinistan trade-union movement to market shellac resins at a capitalist profit margin.

Nicaragua was undoubtedly broke and in debt. The U.S. Empire was its chief creditor, and with events in the Middle East turning strongly anti-U.S., it wasn't doing so well these days either. Had I come to see the effects of revolution, I kept wondering, or a Chapter 11 bankruptcy proceeding?

Revolutionary Nicaragua wanted U.S. dollars, and it stood a chance to get some, as aid and loans, with all kinds of strings attached, of course. If Nicaragua's Third-World friends were able to force devaluation of the dollar as an international trading currency, Nicaraguan planning would be affected negatively, and it would have to turn elsewhere for friendship and financial assistance. Of course, there would also be strings attached to that assistance.

The truth was, I feared, that those who called most strongly for the dissolution of the old U.S. Empire would be hurt badly if that happened.

America claimed to be actively seeking, by friendly means, to make Nicaragua again a client state, but perhaps our hopes and promises, like our dollars, were now in very great trouble throughout the Third World.

Even so, I had no trouble getting my own running-dog-of-Imperialism luggage through customs that first day in Managua. The guards glanced at everything I had, but my own small traveling library of a week-old *Le Monde*, a two-day-old *Uno Mas Uno*, the poems of Vallejo called *Trilce*, and a review-copy of slick Paul Theroux's *The Old Patagonian Express*, was not so much as riffled through by the soldiers or any civilian customs officials.

As I went out afterwards to find a taxi, with my valise straps dangling into the hot bright air of the day, a number of uniformed and well-armed youths were standing next to a jeep finger-popping to Donna Summers' "Love is Such a Beautiful Thing," the fragmentation grenades dangling from their chests reminded me of maracas; and I was rather quickly apprised that the revolution had not, thus far, put an end to begging. A scrawny boy of ten in ragged trousers and a patched shirt the color of dried mouse blood detached himself from a group of armed *milicianos*, and walking toward me in blue rubber flip-flops, asked—with a solemn expression burning beneath his dull-black shock of hair and worried brow—if I had any coins to spare.

He said he just wanted to get food for himself and his brother, a boy a few years older than he, in uniform, who had not been paid in some weeks.

He said they were both pretty far from the home of their parents in Jinotega in the North, where conditions had been very bad throughout the war and there had been much repression and death.

I asked, didn't his brother receive rations from the Sandinistans as a soldier?

"My brother, yes, not me," he said, "and only when he is in his barracks, and since yesterday morning he has been assigned to the airport, and there is no free food here..."

"And you?" I inquired, using the familiar: "What do you do, little friend?"

His face brightened a bit, but then he was stern with me, "What's it your business anyway, meester?"

He started to back away. There was a reek of diesel fumes and burnt volcanic ash, Managua's habitual stench in peace or war.

"I was only asking," I explained.

"So ask. I beg, and I steal if I can and get taxis for people, and then I stay with my brother under the bed in his barracks near the parade ground and the Intercontinental, and since he sometimes has extra food he gives me some..."

I told him to find me a cab and I would give him the few Nicaraguan coins I had. Like many new arrivals, I was still rather short on the local currency.

Waving his hand the boy scampered down the sidewalk toward a battered old green Chevy II. The fenders and side doors were tatooed with bullet holes. Scrambling up from his nap on the front seat, the driver immediately started up his engine and drove toward me.

It turned out I had only three cordobas, less than thirty cents, which I gave to the boy. He thanked me with a small fierce salute, and then held the back door open so I could get inside with my valise and brief case.

"Viva Nicaragua Libre," he told me, with a big grin, as we sped off.

I wondered if he was being facetious.

"About such boys one exercises a little care," my driver (who identified himself as Rigoberto Sarmiento but he said I could call him "the Puma" because of his black coloring and ferocity) immediately declared, at the edge of the parking lot tarmac, as we lurched forward across the *carretera* toward my hotel.

When, out of politeness to this dark man with such a raggedy-brown mustache on his upper lip, I inquired why he thought that way, he merely shrugged and said "why" back at me to mean "because," as if slightly disgusted with his new passenger.

"He got you my business," I reminded the Puma.

"Certainly, such little thieves give Nicaragua Libre a bad name..."

"Not to me," I said.

"But to the world in general..."

Rigoberto said that as a Social Democrat he always had opposed the old government, and he asked if I had heard of the general strike that would soon be taking place.

I reminded him I'd only just arrived.

"Now this is just a rumor," he said, "but it could also very easily happen, for all that I hear, because, you see, we are all so very poor right now that the people could feel restless, and there are just as many rumors as there are bullet holes in this car."

"But nobody knows what to expect," I pointed out.

Rigoberto changed the subject. "Do you write for *Dime* magazine?"

Since I had not even identified myself as a *periodista*-journalist, I told him it was observant of him to guess what I did, but no I never wrote for *Time*, and was not writing, at present, for any other American newspaper or magazine...

"It doesn't take much to recognize you are not from the Red Cross or the World Bank, and what other sort of man who is *gringo*, excuse me sir, would come to Nicaragua at present?"

"True enough..."

"Because you try to speak Spanish," he went on, "though not too badly, so it's important that you listen to the People while you are here and see what you can of the new Nicaragua."

"I always try to do that," I said.

"Look here," Puma Rigoberto said.

We were passing through all that was left of old Managua, after earthquakes and wars, through the barrios that had been most severely afflicted by low-altitude bombing, and rocketry, the months on months of street combat behind barricades of paving stones: barrios Bello Horizonte, Las Americas, Blandon, La Reynaga, and Quinta Niña, the thieves quarter, a little less battered, but splintered from wooden shack to shack, some occasional adobe walls also scored with the marks of tank fire.

And so many thick adobe hovels in ruins, too, roofless, exposed to this rainy season, with pocked walls and broken fencing, and, worse, just empty lots of rubble, crumbling facades. Metal-girdered factories along the way also twisted into contortions.

At every corner as we proceeded toward the devastated center of town which was never restored after the quake of 1973, ragged newsboys in mouse-blood shirts and trousers of grey cotton ticking sold copies of *La Prensa* (now two cordobas, or twenty cents). That courageous daily, whose editor Pedro Joacquin Chamorro had been assassinated, touching off the early indignant stages of the People's insurrection against the Somozas, now had some stern new competition, I had been told, from the lower-priced Sandinistan daily, *Barricada*, (one cordoba) which I'd also heard was being printed on the same machines in the same offices where Somoza had once printed his gruesome propaganda tabloid *Novedades*. (Since writing this I've also heard of another daily by dissident members of the Chamorro family.) Now I saw that *Barricada* (with its *rojonegro* banners) was also being waved at us, as we cruised, by raggedy little boys who were also hawking Chicklets, matches, and Nicaraguan cigarettes.

I asked the Puma which paper he usually preferred to read.

"Naturally, when I can afford it," he told me, "I buy *La Prensa* all the time because you can even get *Barricada* for free sometimes, and it's just the government paper."

"But this is a different government?"

"Maybe so," he said, "all the same it reminds me of

Novedades, under a different name. It's the government paper," he insisted, "and though I support the Junta and there would be no Junta if there were no Sandinistan army, I am the sort of independent man who does not enjoy reading government news."

"And *Barricada* only has government news?"

"It has no other character," he averred. We were caught in a traffic jam of open trucks full of *campesinos* being taken to the rally for Pham Van Dong. "This junta could not last a day without the Sandinistan army, and I support that, you understand, as a Social Democrat, but I don't like to support an official newspaper such as *Barricada*.

"It's like going to church all the time," he went on: "My wife is a Catholic, and I am not, but I respect certain of the priests and even the archbishop some of the time, when they supported us and fought with us they were like us, but I don't like to go and hear their sermons. You understand, I am a man of the world. In the old days I used to spend a good deal of time in Costa Rica."

"I understand," I said, but I was just a little confused.

We had started up again with a lurch and a clank and a grinding of gears behind the diesel pall of many open trucks jammed with people, and Rigoberto told me then how during the last days of the fighting Somoza's National Guard had lined up tanks in front of the offices of *La Prensa*, which he still called the Chamorro paper, after the powerful Nicaraguan clan who still owned it. Though the buildings were protected by large specially-erected steel and concrete barriers, they just could not stand much point-blank artillery fire. Everything was totaled—machinery, archives, offices—out of vengeance and spite and Somoza's personal pique, he insisted.

"Would you care to see just what they did?" he asked me then. Since we were not very far from the ruins, I agreed we should stop there on the way.

"At your service," said the Puma.

Next door to a blue-and-white bullet-riddled Bank-of-America branch office were a small piece of wall, some twists of rusty metal, a few parked wrecks, some piles of rubble, a couple of rusting I-beams, and the metal core of a machine, like an axle, that turned out to be all that was left of *La Prensa*'s presses. Far to the rear stood two small dark prefab buildings with their lights burning.

A peddler had pulled up his cart next to the ruins to vend plastic baggies of Chicha, a pink Nicaraguan soft drink made from herbs and maize.

The Puma said, "With this you have seen all there is to see of what was. But it's possible they will rebuild someday. Undoubtedly," he added.

The peddler said to me, "Buy a Chicha and support Nicaragua Libre."

"Support a peddler," the Puma said.

I was silent, remembering some early mornings in the city room of *La Prensa* when I had gotten tips from that plucky staff about what to expect next in the revolution and by whom. It had been a place of such activity and modernism, in that torpid medieval world.

During some of the fighting, Xavier Chamorro of *La Prensa* had also given me press credentials, which I religiously kept apart from those of the Somoza regime and showed them only when among people I knew to be anti-Somocista.

Now all was in ruins, a hodgepodge of waste, and I wondered aloud how the paper was getting printed and where.

Rigoberto Puma explained that it was all being done in León and then trucked to Managua, except that the writers remained here in the city "in those two little huts you see there, just like always."

"It is a very fine newspaper for Nicaragua," he told me then, "and we are mostly all very proud of it, but I don't always wish to spend the two cordobas, so then I take nothing to read, or I hear the news on the radio. The television is hopeless, just as in Somoza's day, a lot of officials talking."

"Sorry for that," I said.

"Don't have any fear," he added. "Things are better now than they used to be. There's less terror, and there have been no recriminations, except for Macho Negro."

"Macho Negro, the sergeant from Masaya?" I asked.

"You know the very one," he assured me, "and he was tried by a regular Sandinistan tribunal and shot, and even for those others who should have also been shot, it has not happened yet."

"Drive on," I said.

But he remained stalled in front of the ruins.

"Do you know why not?" he asked me.

"Why?"

"Because the people are so generous in victory," he said. "This was a revolution of love."

"And bullets," I assured him.

"Of course, as sure as my fenders," he thumped the outside of his car. "But you know the people are not fools. They all can't read, and some watch televisions, but they have high standards."

"I see."

"And every day it's getting just a little better here," Rigoberto assured me. "There was no food, at first, or very little, and now there's a lot more. Plenty of meat, and even fresh fish, too. There are just so many things we must do, and we have so very little. Nicaragua is..."

"Bankrupt," I interrupted.

"So you know." He accelerated and we moved on. "That's why there will be no general strike right now, but it may happen soon. You will see."

We drove through all the vacant weedy fields in the center of town where people had been living for years in the ruined shells of buildings, and then turned up the hill toward the parade grounds. In front of the lower ramp of the Hotel Intercontinental, Rigoberto told me, as I paid him with some American dollars which he was very glad to have, he hoped to serve me again in Managua. Then he said he would also be very glad to find me a woman should I ever want one (despite the Sandinistans' recent edict against prostitution) or even a boy, if I liked.

I replied, did I seem to be such a fellow?

"It doesn't matter anyway," he said, smiling. "Some people like a *matrimonio* (with a prostitute) and some even like to make love with their mouths, like when you eat a *mamey*, as we call it, and then there are certainly some who like to act like married couples of men."

"It's really all the same ok," he assured me, "except here in Nicaragua we believe with the mouths can cause a lot of stomach cancer so we don't ever do that too much."

My face must have showed my incredulity, for he added, "It's indeed the case, meester. If a woman or a man were to swallow the semen or any of the other fluid from the *mamey*, bad cancer of the stomach would most surely develop."

I pointed out that sounded more like superstition than fact, and hoped the new government would be offering sex education to the people in the future. I got out of the cab, thanked him again for trying to serve me in so many ways, and reached for his hand and shook it.

"Next time we meet," said the Puma, "I shall have a much better car than this . . . a 1966 Chevrolet Impala with air conditioning. You'll see."

I said I would be very glad for that.

"Well then thanks," he told me, "and we'll meet again, and if I can ever serve you with a boy or a woman . . ."

"Before you said a woman or a boy."

"Either way you like it," he told me, "Though not for love of God with the mouth . . . like a priest, for Christ's sake."

"Christ has nothing to do with it."

"Agreed. And neither should you," he told me: "Agreed?"

The door slammed. As he drove off, the car rattled and shook down the ramp toward the wastelands of old Managua.

I stood alone with my valise. Fresh from the presses, a pile of *Barricadas* lay stacked up on the sidewalk in front of the glass entranceway to the hotel. The inch-thick red-and-black banner on each framed two cameos: one of General Sandino and another of a street fighter in a beret firing his weapon behind a waist-high pile of "Somoza-block" paving stones.

Underneath was the legend: "Year of the Liberation," and the price: one cordoba (about ten cents).

A chunky dark man edged toward me then to ask if I would sell him some dollars, any amount I had on me, and he would give me such a very good price, twice as much or more than the official rates. But I had given my last few singles to the Puma, Rigoberto.

Then fortunately, the hotel bellhop emerged. Recognizing me from my last visit, he greeted me, effusively, in English, so that my persistent currency speculator seemed startled, and drew back a moment: "Welcome back Señor Elman..."

"It's good to be back in Free Nicaragua."

"It's good to have you back in Free Nicaragua."

"It's even good to have you tell me that," I said, still struggling to equal all his effusiveness.

The man who wished to trade was back at my other side, now offering me two-and-one-half times the legal rate of exchange.

"It's not illegal yet," said the bellhop, "so go ahead if you like."

I figured he must be in on the deal, and I was stalling. I really didn't wish to trade. I knew the Junta was trying to control black marketeering and profiteering, even if trading dollars still wasn't illegal.

The bellhop started off for the lobby with my bags, while, embarrassed, I found myself glancing down at my feet at the columns of photos and type in *Barricada*, past the smiling carved ivory features of Pham Van Dong as he was caught by a telephoto lens stepping down out of an Aeroflot jet onto a salvaged old Pan Am gangway, and then a particular paragraph caught my eye.

It just floated about on the page in the sharpest black and white that the Socialist Party was meeting to consider dissolving itself so as to become a part of the vanguard Sandinistan National Front movement.

"Welcome to Pham Van Dong," I said aloud.

There was band music and cheering reaching my ears from far away. Down the hill, in the Plaza of the Revolution, not too far from Managua's lone skyscraper, the white Bank-of-America building, Pham Van Dong was probably even now addressing a large crowd of Sandinistan officials and people who had all been ferried in from the countryside to the rally.

My bellboy returned. Was I planning to check in right now, he wished to know, or would I go down the hill to observe the "manifestation" with all the rest of the people?

I thought I would unpack first.

"There'll be another some other day," he said. "Today is a historic moment for Nicaragua Libre but now almost every day in the week there is something, or some leader from someplace strange is here."

"Three times ten," said the trader to my right. "I can do no better than that."

But I told the man I had nothing to sell and went inside.

Epitaph for the Somozas

"Your carcasses must not profain this earth."
—Mario Cajina Vega

Marco's Story

"**Y**ou know, Rick, I fought —I had to fight," Marco told me, on greeting me, at last, in person with a hug that first Sunday of my return after the war in the town of Masaya "because it was a matter of life and death. But as I am not really a soldier so they made me quartermaster..."

My friend was smiling so that the little scar on his forehead between his eyes from the days when he had been tortured by Somoza's soldiers was just a deep crease.

He was large, coppery-skinned, heavy-chested, and now he limped a little. We stood beneath a spread of gnarled shade trees in the little park opposite the former National Guard fort, now rubble, in Masaya's main square, and when I offered him a cigarette, still scarce and expensive in Nicaragua, he took one and told me, "The Indians from Monimbo—they were the ones who captured this *cuartel*. When you were here the first time it was mostly the young men from the towns who fought and they were brave but eventually they had to give up and flee to the hills. But the Indians they could not flee, and they fought to the last man."

"You should have seen them, Rick, men against tanks and armored cars." Shuddering a bit, he added, "The little three-inch guns on the armored cars they're no big problem, but the Sherman tanks have big cannons and machine guns...and even so these Indians they fought like hell. You have a word for it in English, I believe: *hombre...masculinidad*...no, manhood, I think you would say. They fought with manhood here in Masaya, Rick," enunciating each English syllable with evident care and pride, "and so many died, one over the body of the next."

I met Marco in the middle of the first battle of Masaya when I sought refuge in his house from the shooting on the streets. A writer, hardly a warrior, although a man of strong sentiments, jailed and tortured by the previous regime many times for his activities, he had sometimes been impoverished, and had to live in exile. During the fighting, he had sent his eldest children abroad so they would not be murdered by Somoza's Guardia, and he was proud to tell me again how in the end, at 48, he too had fought and was wounded.

We had taken a coffee together at his house, and now he insisted that we walk about his ruined old city so that he could tell me more of the battles, and even show me how well the prisoners were being treated in the fortress of Coyatepe.

It was the National Day, commemorating Nicaragua's independence from Spain, but given special importance this year by the liberation. Most of the people in the town still seemed to be asleep at eleven in the morning, though some were at work in their nearby fields of corn and beans.

Marco told me, "Right now there's enough to eat for everybody, but drinking remains a problem with the Sandinistans. One can get arrested for being publicly drunk, and so one tries to be very careful. Do you like Rum Plata, Rick?"

Before I could reply, he answered, "That's all the rum there is, white rum, at present, so later with lunch we'll drink, but right now it doesn't matter very much what we drink later because there really isn't anything else."

"As you say."

"A pleasure," he assured me, his face full of sudden brightness, his English somewhat more stilted than usual.

There were tears in his eyes. He pointed down toward a tiny orange metal bridge across a ditch at the entrance to the city.

"Beautiful," he announced. Here his comrades and the townspeople had fought to the death to keep the army from crossing, so that they were never able to retake Masaya. Despite days and nights of artillery fire from the citadel of Coyatepe, high above the town, and pinpoint bombing by helicopters with 500-pound projectiles, the people held the town. Marco said, "They could not get across."

"It was some fighting here," he added.

We were peering down into a gulley where a number of small cars still lay in wreckage.

Marco said, "Across the highway they shot down a private plane bringing supplies to us from Costa Rica. You can see the wreck, if you like."

"Those were such days and nights," he went on, nostalgically. "We seemed to be all alone in the world, just those of us here who fought and died."

He wiped a glob of wetness from the corner of his eye. Marco was limping quite a bit as we started to go back toward the Indian village of Monimbo, and he told me now everybody was as before. There was even a certain distrust again, though not as bad as before. It had to do with "the Cubans" who had come to town to aid in the reconstruction. Some people just didn't trust them. They did not mind if they were doctors, because doctors were needed, but some were in the schools, he'd been told, "teaching Marxism," and many people were not happy about that.

"And you?" I asked. "How do you feel?"

"I am a Nicaraguan," he said fiercely. "I'm not against Cuba and I'm not against the U.S. This is my only country. I fought for it...you tell people that."

We started to walk again. Passing the broken shops of

woodworkers and shoemakers, metalsmiths and weavers, Marco waved to certain stoic brown faces in doorways. They were his old comrades; some shouted back or waved at him. But every few yards on a wall was a scribble in paint or marking pen, a few words in memorial to one of those hundreds of men and women who had fallen in Masaya and Monimbo. The names were preceded by *Comandante* and afterwards came the declaration: *Presente!*, and sometimes there were also to be seen the faint traces of green crosses inside circles where Somoza's soldiers had fallen earlier in the war.

Abruptly Marco pointed toward a large dark-brown mound of barren earth which must have once been occupied by a building of considerable size.

"Here a 500-pound bomb fell point blank," he said, "and maybe twenty people were killed..."

He told me then it would probably cost more than $30,000,000 to restore his city as it once was, according to estimates, and "of course the money will be needed for more important things. But it was such a pretty place once. Do you remember?"

"When I was here there was fighting," I reminded him.

"Still it was pretty until the last few months of the war," he told me. "Then..."

He stopped himself again. We had come to the war museum in Monimbo and there were many young Sandinistan *milicianos* standing about in arms, boys and girls, and they were chatting gaily with some of the local people.

Down the block stood a tall lean pale person in a suit jacket and open white shirt. He was recognized by Marco who approached him and they talked together. Then the two came my way, and my friend said, "It so happens he too is called Marco and he is my old schoolfriend. He has such a terrible headache because he drank too much last night, so we will go together with him later to take something for his 'cat's skull,' what you call 'hair of the dog'..."

A few steps later, he told me, "Marco was a justice of the

peace for a little while under Somoza but as he has always aspired to being a just man he had to resign a few years back, and as you can tell he is not afraid of coming down to Monimbo with us today."

We had come to a small private house with an iron gate in front. A short woman came to the gate and opened it for us. She was the curator of this strange museum of rusty ancient sporting rifles, homemade contact bombs, and hand-fashioned stove-pipe mortars, all devised by the Indians of Monimbo to fight against the well-trained and well-equipped National Guard of the Somozas.

Marco had asked her to bring them out from their closets to display before me, and she cradled them all to her bosom, held very close inside her arms, like infants, though each was heavy with dust and corrosion.

I told both Marcos it was doubtful such weaponry could ever be used again, unless it was better cared for.

My friends just laughed: "They have much better weapons now, these Indians, and they will never need these again," and then I remembered the noises made by a sound truck in a nearby coffee-growing town I had visited only the day before, the very day I'd arrived. The sound truck had gone about the village pleading and cajoling with its citizenry to turn in all pistols and small arms at the Sandinistan *cuartel*; even then I had thought to myself that that seemed such a highly unlikely thing for them to do, after so much recent Nicaraguan history.

The woman was taking all the weapons back to her closet, as if putting a baby to bed for the night, and my friend Marco said, "This victory was a gift to all of us here from the young and *these* people of Monimbo, who fought and suffered such terrible losses. Now we need to reconstruct and yet maintain Nicaragua..."

Later over an ample lunch of stewed goat, boiled squash, and rice, in the house he shared with six other refugees' families, I watched Marco chatting with his young daughters as they returned in their school uniforms from morning classes. There were certain errands to be done. It was all very normal, or returning to normalcy.

The girls, in first womanhood, were pretty and willowy, with expressions of serenity seemingly undisturbed by the months of constant fighting.

One of the women in Marco's temporary house ran a beauty parlor; another sold elaborate celebratory cakes she baked and decorated. The house was cluttered and busy; after lunch Marco's mother took a chair and sat under the eaves near the sidewalk with some older lady friends and leisurely drank coffee and gossiped as they had not been able to do in quite some time, I was sure.

But one of the middle-aged female refugees was very silent whenever she was spoken to. Her face was without expression and, even when I asked her politely where I could go to wash my hands before eating, she said nothing, as if she were being rude or did not even hear me.

I asked Marco about her as we walked to the café for a bottle of Rum Plata.

It was serious, he told me, but nothing I need fret about personally. This woman was just very sick from all the bombings and shootings, and she had been that way ever since the war.

She must have been very badly frightened, he said, because she kept silent and did not seem to hear people, and the doctors said nothing could be done. She would either get well or remain that way. She helped with chores in the kitchen, but "she could not be spoken to or approached."

"Maybe she will be better again," he said, "but we can't tell. There is simply no room for people like her in the hospitals, and there are still many like her in Nicaragua."

Before leaving the house, I had asked him if, after the bombings, he had been able to savage anything from his house that he had particularly treasured, and he nodded and led me to an airtight glass bookcase, and removed from the bottom shelf a wooden tray of movable type, beautifully fabricated out of wood and cast lead. "I had them made for me especially in Holland for my press, which is no more. It all happened so long ago..."

He showed off the various fonts and allowed me to pick them up in my hands and feel their weight and inspect their design before returning them to their resting place again.

But now in the café, over rum, Marco grew talkative about the old days, when he'd had his press: "We were very young and very idealistic, Rick. We all hated old Somoza, but very few of us then were willing to do anything about it. During those years I ran a small weekly newspaper and I was arrested six times by the police, who were soldiers, and each time they were right, I suppose, because I *was* plotting against them, in a way, just as they always suspected, but as I would tell them nothing, and as they really knew very little about me and my friends, I was just tortured."

"Once," he went on, "for twenty-six days I was kept in a cell with only bread and water and nobody to talk to, and then one night they came for me and blindfolded me and took me to some fields beyond town in a jeep. There was a lieutenant in charge and he asked me to get down out of the jeep and relieve myself but I couldn't. You see, I was much too frightened. I just could not urinate. I stayed inside that jeep...

"Well again they pleaded with me to relieve myself and he told me they would not harm me, but I was just too frightened.

"We stayed that way in the dark in those fields many hours and I don't even know why to this day, except maybe they wanted to say they had killed me trying to escape, and after a while they brought me back to my cell, and then I was released.

"I still don't know why. I *was* plotting with some young army officers (it was the time of 'old' Somoza), but they didn't know that, Rick, because those officers were not harmed. They only thought it was so because, you know, my newspaper seemed to know so many things, and so they arrested me, and then after a while they let me go, after a month, because there was no way they could know

...How could they? But they gave me this scar on my forehead.

"For a while then, like now, it was hard to work or even think straight, and then..."

"Rick," he interrupted himself, to smile at me benignly so that that cicatrix in his forehead deepened, "that was so long ago. But now we have a new Nicaragua Libre. Let's drink to that..."

He poured both of us another glass of white rum.

When I left my friend that evening, we were both a little drunk. We had gone up to the fortress at Coyatepe, built by United States marines for Somoza in the '30s, and walked about its battlements, and afterwards Marco introduced me to some of the small garrison of young men on duty there, and to some prisoners of the new government who were engaged in doing fatigue duties, but were living very much like the garrison itself.

A prisoner was pulling water up from a well, and Marco told me he was a famous "ear" who had informed on the Sandinistans and been responsible for many deaths.

The prisoner glanced away; he was a short slightly-hunchbacked fellow with a very ugly, almost-simian face, and when he saw I was smoking asked me for a cigarette.

I had only one left.

"Give it to him anyway," Marco said. "It's not easy the life he has to lead now."

I gave away my last cigarette and then we headed drunkenly down toward the town and the bus station. There were Sandinistan patrols on some of the streets, and under Marco's guidance we walked away from them.

"You should be very careful around your hotel, too," Marco said. "There are Cuban security people everywhere. And be careful with whom you speak. The country now is free, but not everybody thinks it is. Next time you come to Nicaragua," he added, then, "I will try to find you a room in the house of a friend."

We'd come to the new marketplace. The old had burned

down in crossfires during the fighting. This new make-shift place of stands of scrap wood was peopled by women selling cheap leather and cotton souvenirs of the fighting: belts, scarves, wallets, pocketbooks—all illustrated with the cameo grin of Sandino in those *rojonegro* colors.

Marco said, "I wish you could have seen my city before the war."

"It was even pretty when I saw it," I said, "though there was fighting."

"Maybe someday you think there will be a way to make it pretty again?"

I climbed aboard a bus that was nearly filled from front to back and, leaning far out over the roadway as we began to move along, shook my friend's hand for the last time.

"We'll talk, Marco," I said, "and you'll come to see me in Managua."

"Sooner or later," he said, "one way or the other. Just be careful Rick." And then he turned, slowly and heavily, and limped his way back through the ruined old market-place toward his family.

"The revolution is the Indian.
It's a book, and a free man."
—From **Cartel** by Mario Cajina Vega

"This is what the antediluvian beast (Somoza) desires:
the liver of a pickled child,
the milk of the pus of a syphilitic prostitute,
the testicles of an unbathed insurrectionist,
the menstruation of a virgin,
the genital saliva of a priest,
the urine and diarrhea of poets.
With this menu he could live and die anywhere
except in Nicaragua where his mother bore him...
—**From "Antes Del Sabado," by Ernesto Mejia Sanchez**
(as printed in La Prensa, reprinted by permission of the
author)

A Sunday after the War

The newspapers exhorted and cajoled; there was very little real news every day except how so many workers in the meat trade or the bottling industry were donating all of one day's pay, or two, to rebuild a school or an infirmary. I really couldn't see much point in that, with so many people still driving about Managua in Mercedes Benzes; and if you took from the small, wealthy, entrepreneurial class everybody else would be just that much poorer for lack of business managers. Decisions were being made behind closed doors by the higher Sandinistan cells and the Junta, but one thing seemed pretty clear: Nicaragua still seemed to need its well-to-do business class to stimulate what was left of its economy.

The country was just so poor, and getting even poorer. It had changed because the Somozas had fled, taking nearly all that wasn't nailed in place with them. But, at least, there was no more National Guard terror. People were constantly assuring themselves of that. They openly confided to one another that this change had indeed occurred, as if pinching themselves in public. And for the rest there was just the grinding daily existence: poverty and want and unemployment and so much more hard work to do, just to get by, to pay back debts. It was like winning at tennis and being told you had to pay for the balls, for your game, and all the games ever played beforehand. People shrugged their shoulders; we won't pay back our debts. Yet schools, post offices, hospitals, sewers, and water systems were needed, and there was no other available financing. Housing was in short supply; the dead must be reburied. How would all of this be paid for except through more loans?

In *Barricada*, Nicaragua's great poet, Ernesto Cardenal, now Minister of Culture, reported daily on his recent trip to Iran to chat with the Ayatollah Khomeini. Without much humor, this renegade Catholic father compared all the ways the two revolutions were similar, but, frankly, I hoped they were not. I couldn't tell if Cardenal had turned in his sense of irony when he was given his government portfolio, but I really felt relieved every time I passed one of those huddles of heavily-armed young people and overheard them singing along to "Saturday Night Fever."

On the first Sunday, after arriving in Nicaragua, I hitched a ride from the outskirts of Managua more than halfway to León, to the little town of La Paz Centro, aboard the back of an open white Toyota pickup truck driven by a Sandinistan comandante. He had his wife and three-year-old daughter along. They sat up front; his *galil* assault rifle, which he kept with its stock and tripod folded, rattling across his lap.

I sat in the open back because there was no more room in the cab of the little pickup. There were just a few bags of fertilizer and a long dun-colored roll of dirty tarpaulin in the back with me, when we took off on the road that went past the municipal aqueduct.

It was a muggy day, the sun in and out and then in again behind some clouds over Lake Managua. My comandante driver was a fine-looking dark man with a broad chest and defiant black mustaches. He looked like a cattleman, a rangy person, wore the sort of faded tubular Western-style jeans and boots over his long legs and big feet that hinted he may have spent a lot of his life on horseback.

He was probably no more than thirty, and his wife looked even younger, soft and brown. She wore a faded blue sundress that showed off her round and pretty shoulders, and over her hair was a blue kerchief of the same material tied beneath her chin. Their little girl of five, who cuddled silently on her lap, also wore a *pañuelo* around her head tied out of the comandante's *rojonegro* scarf.

This wasn't the first or last time I would drive with an armed person in Free Nicaragua. Managua was still not entirely safe at night from roving bands of former paramilitaries who had not yet been apprehended, I was told, so that sometimes, after dark, the noise of gunfire would be loud and frightening. Meeting people during the day who were armed, I hoped they had their safety catches in place; for some of the younger people used to play with their weapons and swing them about jauntily; and accidents could be too easily fatal: a weapon such as a *galil*, for example, can fire off its clip of thirty-or-so bullets in one short squeeze and burst.

The comandante and his wife were very friendly people. They asked where I was from and did not frown excessively when I told them "The States."

We shared my cigarettes, and I gave a bit of foil-wrapped chocolate I had in my shirt pocket to their little girl.

Once we were on the highway the woman squirmed about because we were driving against the wind. When we stopped for a red light, she explained in a loud voice that they were going on to León on a family matter, but they would also be coming back before dark to Managua. If I cared to wait for them for a ride home, I should be in front of the big restaurant on the highway at La Paz Centro around 5:30 in the evening.

The light changed, and we drove on through the outskirts of Managua and into the lush open countryside.

The highway we drove on was very badly chewed from tank caterpillar treads, and rocket and bomb explosions. Although the comandante tried to swerve around as many potholes as possible, there was two-way traffic, and he often could not. Bouncing up and down painfully hard against the floor of the truck, I felt quite precarious in the back, even when I wasn't bouncing, while we drove past thick meadows and hedgerows of shrubs and trees in that otherwise seemingly-deserted countryside. Supposing one of those phantom detachments of Guardia deserters lurked nearby?

The sun came out rather strongly after a while, a silvery disk against a lining of soft yellowish cumulus clouds, and it made me squint and sweat. I could see actual rays beaming down onto the deep-green earth. Over Momotombo volcano was a rainbow, and the foot of one of its arcs seemed to be planted in a big city across the lake. We were driving along the opposite shore of the huge lake now, which was hung with a thin scrim-like mist, as in some Chinese or Japanese woodcuts. In the shallows of the lakeside squatted *campesinos* planting rice or harvesting it; I couldn't tell.

At Nagarote, the comandante stopped his truck once more, for an Indian woman carrying some reed baskets.

She climbed aboard the back by herself and sat down opposite me, on top of the tarpaulin, her long dark skirt covering her legs which had showed just barely as she climbed aboard; and then, without my asking, declared she too was going to La Paz because there was to be a fiesta in the afternoon. Did I know about the fiesta?

I confessed I did not.

Where was I from?

I confessed again to the States, as if I couldn't have guessed from her stares that she knew.

The woman nodded, darkly, glumly. Shouting above the wind, she asked if I would like to see a picture of her little brother.

When I said yes, she reached inside the pocket of her skirt, and produced a Polaroid color print of a corpse, supine, naked from the waist up, with a small dark bullet hole in his forehead.

That face was stained with blood the color of grape juice. It was certainly not at peace, at rest. Twisted into a grimace by so much sudden pain, the lips had sprung apart; there was a row of fierce teeth, as in some sport fish after they have been hooked.

Shuddering, I looked away and handed the photograph back.

"How did your brother die?" I inquired, though probably I meant to say "when."

"In the struggle," she explained, "the fighting." Her voice was harsh. She remained dry-eyed and glum, as if just cross, rather than grieving: "My brother was a hero, a martyr of the revolution."

"So many were. Of course."

"It was maybe the day before Somoza finally left Nicaragua. The people said he had gone off to Guatemala that day for assistance, but, as there was still some Guardia in one of the outposts near Nagarote, they came in to our village to find trucks so they could escape to Honduras.

"Suddenly everybody started shooting," she went on. "My brother told them to surrender, but The Tiger, for that's what people called him, he shot my brother anyway with his pistol, and then the people shot him . . .

"He lost his life when the war was almost finished," she continued, "but it could have happened to him even earlier. He was a Sandinistan . . . "

Her face looked tight and warped, dark with blood; she presented it chin first toward the wind and blinked as a cinder touched one of her eyes.

"A martyr," she repeated, as we rounded the last steep pass at the entrance to La Paz Centro, and stopped short in the roadway for two scrawny gray Cebu cattle to cross from one side to the other.

In town the comandante stopped his truck again in front of one of the potter's stalls, got out of the cab, and walked slowly around to the back, with his weapon slung, and opened up the tailgate for us so we did not have to climb out.

We both helped the woman with her baskets; she didn't even stop to say thanks, but started down toward the entrance to the village square.

The comandante, so tall and lean, asked me for another cigarette.

"This is a nice little place, La Paz," he told me then, "and I hope you will enjoy yourself here. If I had the time to stay we would. Everybody can use a fiesta sometimes, believe me."

"That would certainly be very nice," I told him.

"My wife must see to certain family business, so of course we can't." Again he hoisted his *galil* up to his shoulder so that its folding stock banged against the tailgate of the truck, loudly. I offered him more cigarettes for the remainder of his trip, but he declined. He didn't wish to get used to smoking again, since cigarettes were expensive and bad for your health anyway. As they drove off along the blacktop in the direction of León, the comandante's wife and child waved back at me.

It must have just stopped raining very heavily in La Paz because both dirt shoulders of the paved highway were mucky. A few barefoot kids stood up to their ankles in the puddles, cooling their feet. The sun had now gotten much warmer, brighter. The moment I was set down in La Paz, I began to sweat.

Loping slowly down the road, six horsemen on small gray-and-brown ponies tricked out with black leather and silver studs headed my way.

One of the men wore a felt slouch hat and dangled a lasso by his side, and as they all came abreast of each other in the roadway, their horses' flanks steaming and twitching, they seemed rather elegant, their gaily beribboned cruppers bobbing. The small men sat smooth in their thin leather saddles, a party of locals in full regalia for a fiesta. But just when I thought they might be passing my way, they veered around to the left in a file, toward the center of the village, some two or three hundred yards down this muddy dirt track.

The Indian woman at the pottery stand, where I was, told me she had some very inexpensive things to sell, if I was interested.

I told her I was afraid to buy any of her fragile delicately-turned pots, for fear they would break before I could ever get them back to my home in the States.

"Have no fear," she said. "I'll wrap them for you in a newspaper."

She was dangling a few large sheets of *Barricada*. I knew better, declined the bargain, fearing breakage and moved on.

Many cars were parked in front of the various traveler's restaurants at La Paz. Trucks and buses also kept stopping to let their passengers off. The little blue shack where the National Guard used to man a machine-gun post was pocked and deserted. On its front wall were scribbled the names of those who had fallen to capture it.

It was in La Paz, I remembered, that the first U.S. Marines in Nicaragua were killed by a Sandinistan ambush. In 1926, a captain and a private were surprised by seventy-five armed *campesinos* behind barricades in the village square, a long-time stronghold of revolutionary sentiments.

But now, across from me in a tiny meadow on the other side of the highway, about ten young boys in bright blue flannel baseball uniforms with scarlet trim bought ice cream sticks from a peddler. A car door slammed, and I flinched. The boys began to giggle.

"Hey Yankee," one called out, more in amusement than hostility "what you scared about?"

His *compañeros* were laughing.

They had already finished their game, and their dark narrow faces under their peaked caps glistened from sweat. With the sudden outpouring of sunlight, they seemed like such a gaudy bunch, all day-glo blue and scarlet, even down to their socks, against the intense greens of that meadow.

One boy waved a black aluminum baseball bat at me and shouted: "P*eee*tsburgh Pirates."

All the other kids cheered.

I started on my way again through town and heard the rude squealing of a siren, coming closer and closer, from the direction of Managua, and sensed trouble.

I got behind one of the parked buses in front of the restaurant just as this van came down the street with its loudspeakers blaring from little horns overhead that pointed in all directions: "*Atención Atenci...*"

The words crackled with static and were not easy to decipher: "*Compañeros de La Paz Centro,*" I heard, and then a lot of what seemed like the proper names for animals.

This was a circus come to entertain the people of the countryside for the next week or so.

Their truck proceeded to the very edge of town and then came back again and did the tour once more, before accelerating off again in the direction of León.

Under the thatched roof of La Casa Tropica, in the high airy space beneath the rafters, a juke box blared out mambo music. Woodsmoke combined with the rich smells of stewing meats. There were many bottles of Toño and Victoria beer on each table. A few couples danced slow and close together, as if caught up in the same weave of woodsmoke and stewing-meat smells. Behind his counter stood the big patron taking cash, and some young women from the village acted as waitresses; they, too, wore baseball caps. In the wide open doorway a couple of ragged little boys begged the various diners for coins.

Nearly all the tables were occupied by large families from the neighboring cities, and they all seemed to be having a pleasant time together, as if just being easy and relaxed with each other, for the moment, were a sufficient reward after so many years of oppression and bloodshed. I saw a nearly-vacant corner table and asked the man who was sitting there if I could join him.

Without looking up from his plate of food, he nodded assent.

He was a young slim fellow, nattily dressed in fitted double-knit slacks, and a white ruffled *guayabera* shirt that had its sleeves rolled up to show off his heavy weight-lifter's biceps. On one finger of the hand in which he held his fork was a gold class ring from a university.

When I asked for a gourd of chilled cacao from the waitress, the fellow finally glanced up and inquired in good English if I had been very long in Nicaragua.

I explained it was not my first trip.

The man leaned further across our table to ask in a whisper—though he was not doing anything illegal—if I had some dollars to trade.

I didn't and I was apologetic about that.

"It doesn't matter," he said. "There is really nothing I could do with such money here in Nicaragua."

"Most people who want such money are planning to leave," I pointed out.

"I am a Nicaraguan. Why should I leave?"

He seemed to be implying that others should, but not he, and I was glad to hear such sentiments expressed, though I said nothing more.

"Nevertheless," he suddenly told me, "I am really bored with myself now that the war is over. That's why I came here today. Sometimes in the old days you could meet women here. In my city now there's nothing to be done on Sundays. In the cinema they are showing a Cuban film on how to read and write, but I already know how so I can't go to any movies."

His grin interrupted the somber cast of his face. "That's why I thought I should look for a woman here today. Because my balls are very heavy, you understand?

"As you say..." he added.

I nodded.

We were staring into the air, without anything to say.

I asked, "Were you one of the fighters?"

"I am an agronomist of cotton, and that is also important to do. Only this year," he added, "as you must know, the cotton could not be planted."

"So I've heard."

"Such a victory was important, and it makes me proud," he said then, "but the war was a terrible disaster for this country. I am very, very sorry."

Without another word said, he got up and went over toward the juke box where a dark slim young woman was peering at the various selections.

I watched them start to converse as easily as anywhere else in the world, I thought, and then my waitress came by with my cacao, and when I looked again they had gone elsewhere. Disappeared out the door onto the patio. A middle-aged matron sat down opposite me, and when the waitress cleared her place she asked in Spanish if I was from Managua.

I told her the States.

She told me quickly then who she was, though I forget now, from a very important old family. Her cousin was Sacasa, the Ambassador. Her mother and Yoyo—old Somoza's mother...*Cousins*...Did I understand? Would I care to sit with her family at that big table in the corner and have a coffee?

She pointed over toward a table in the darkest side of the room where a number of men in suits and ties and ladies in dark silk dresses were all peering my way.

I declined immediately, saying I wished to go off to the village to see the fiesta.

She asked me next if I had any dollars to trade.

Again I told her no I did not.

In heavily accented English, she said: "It's worse now here than before. In Granada the upstarts took over our club. Don't believe people who tell you things are better. Come to see us in Managua. We live in Altogracia. Everybody knows the name..."

But she never got a chance to tell me her name. I got up and left some coins on the table and started for the door.

"I was here before," I told her, as I left. "I don't remember any paradise then."

On my way toward the village square I couldn't help but take notice once again of all the holes and chasms in the adobe walls of the houses of La Paz Centro.

In many places, no walls were left standing, just tumbles of rubble and splintered wood.

The sun was out now so brightly that people stuck their heads out doors as if to bathe their faces in its warmth, and, perhaps, follow my progress toward the square itself, as I had attracted a number of young beggars who were trailing behind me.

At last, when I stopped and distributed some few cordobas, feeling again very self-conscious about such a dubious largesse, I saw an old man sprawled drunkenly on the sidewalk, not five paces from where I stood.

He had his fly open; he was damp all over, and he was groaning: *"Comandante... ay comandante, salva..."*

"Yo no soy comandante," I assured him.

"Comandante... comandante..."

It was the only word he seemed able to mutter, and it wasn't clear any longer if it was directed at me or at the bright dusty air of the lane itself.

Abruptly, his daughter emerged from one of those small dark houses, and she pulled at his trousers, to urge him to get up and go inside. He would get into trouble for being so soused in public.

"Papa andalo papa, por favor, please walk," she kept repeating, but he could not be moved, and he would say nothing more.

A young man in a *rojonegro* scarf joined them. He carried a .45 caliber pistol in a holster, and after looking the situation over, he pointed it at me, and said to the girl: "Take him inside. Not in front of the North Americans. We don't like such things seen," as if entirely unaware I could understand Spanish.

At once he grabbed the old man by his shoulders to help the girl, and they started to drag this old man along the ground. He had begun to groan again, but I could not make out what he was saying, and went on my way again, feeling bad for the girl and for being where I shouldn't have been, but not really wishing to leave.

In the principal square, a few hundred people had assembled behind some barricades. There must have been thirty horsemen rigged out as if for a rodeo, and behind a low-fenced palisade was another scrawny grey Cebu bull, taller than any of the horses.

They were all here to take part in the fiesta, but the band had not yet arrived from Managua, and everybody was getting just a little impatient, restless.

Some vendors went about the crowd selling drippy ice creams, fruit, tacos dipped in cheese.

The woman next to me declared: "This fair can't possibly begin until all the horses arrive."

"Those are horses..." I pointed, "over there."

"Those are just ponies," she declared. "I mean *los grandes*...Cuban horses...*machos*...with Arabian blood and steel turrets and great big guns..."

"She's just crazy," the man next to her told me.

I said, "You call tanks horses..."

"We all call them shit," she said, "but they are sometimes necessary, and if you gringos won't sell them to us we'll go to Russia...or maybe the Cubans will..."

"If they had them to sell," I said.

She frowned at me darkly: "Politics can ruin a fiesta ...however, this will be a regular fiesta, and we are all friends here in La Paz after the liberation, and later they will kill that skinny gray bull you see over there and roast it on an open fire so that everybody can have some."

"He's a real bull, isn't *she*?" she demanded of me then. "Can't you just taste his balls?"

I wasn't sure how to reply.

"A real skinny bull," she said: "*Flacco*...we will have them don't you worry..." and she laughed harshly.

I asked her when she thought the band might arrive.

"When they feel like coming," she told me, "but they have promised to stay a long long time."

I excused myself from her company and started strolling about the square.

The old Guardia *cuartel* was now a *miliciano* headquarters and tribunal. There was a stenciled notice tacked to its front veranda. The people were advised not to loiter there if they lacked official business.

The belltower of the old church across the way had also been hit, as if it had once served as a sniper post, which many of course did; a few of the other buildings around the square had also been totally leveled by artillery or bombs.

On the street behind the *cuartel* was a headquarters of the Sandinistan youth organization. They occupied a large wooden building fitted out like an auditorium, with a stage, flanked by big pictures of General Sandino and Che Guevara.

I entered the hall and noticed that a meeting of some youngsters was taking place around a table in the room adjacent to the main entranceway.

My footsteps must have echoed much too loudly against the wooden floors because that meeting quickly broke up, and then all the youngsters presented themselves to me in a group behind their leader, a tall boy of sixteen with a *rojonegro* arm band.

What did I want?

Young people that age in Nicaragua were among the fiercest of the insurgents; I felt I had intruded on a private self-criticism meeting and wanted to be careful about what I said, because I didn't care to be misinterpreted.

I tried to explain I was just walking around in this town where I had been before.

"You have no real business here?" The youth asked, flatly, more like an assertion than a question.

I nodded. I had no business I could think of except that I was a friend of Nicaragua, and a writer.

A very pretty girl with shiny brown cheeks asked me very loudly in English: "*Vat* is your name?"

"Richard," I said. "My name is Richard..."

"That's all I know English," she giggled at me, as if to provoke me: "*Vat* is your name is all I know."

And she merged with the group again.

I turned away to the young man who seemed to be their leader.

"I really didn't mean to interrupt what was going on. I was just looking around..."

"If you have no real business here," the young man said, with a quiet ferocity, "now you must go."

I went back out to the square. The band still had not yet arrived. It was very very hot out now, and there was hardly any shade under the trees that was not occupied by large families of picnicking villagers.

A couple of horsemen trotted up on sleek beautiful full-sized brown horses, and tied their long reins to the palisade.

A friend had told me that after the Somocistas fled Nicaragua a lot of the peasants were able to liberate some very beautiful ranch animals.

Next to me a couple stood with their arms about each others' waists. I heard the man ask the woman if she wanted to come back to his house for a little while.

She said, "There'll be time enough for that after the fiesta."

"But I am going to work early."

"Nobody works after one of these."

"Nowadays we do," the man said, and then his face got cross as he saw me looking at them.

It was getting late, and I was just a little hungry. I started down the other road from town toward the highway on which all the restaurants and pottery stands of La Paz were located.

La Casa Tropica had emptied out. It was nearly vacant. I found a table near the door and asked the patron's wife, who came to me immediately, for a plate of stew and a bottle of Victoria beer.

When she brought the food, I grabbed her gently by the arm and asked if she remembered me from the time of the war.

"Oh yes," she said, "I remember because you were among the journalists and your hand always shook when you drank cacao."

After lunch I bought a few shallow bowls at the potter's stand for two dollars a piece. It seemed the only friendly conversations I could have would cost money in La Paz Centro today.

The potter's wife complimented me on my Spanish as she wrapped my bowls in paper; even so one had broken by the time I was back in my hotel in Managua.

That afternoon darkened and steamed a little. The weather was changing again. There would probably be more rain. I didn't like the idea of returning to Managua after dark, and I felt so lonely and isolated among all the Sunday activities of the people of La Paz Centro.

It wasn't really unfriendliness I experienced, but a lack of positive feeling toward me, of friendliness. People just seemed to have no time for strangers. They took my money and went about their business without any care for me, enjoying the freedom of the day for as long as it would last.

In the days before, when there had been fighting, they had pleaded with me and others to tell some of their ordeal to the world, but that world had not really cared that much to hear; and now that these people were victorious anyway, they were trying to live and reconstruct and perhaps transform their social order.

From the village square came the sound of firecrackers going off, many at a time, and I recognized that spattering noise, so different from gunfire, for exactly what it was, as I recalled one of the sieges of Masaya when the rebels had surrounded the Guard *cuartel* in August, 1978 and had set off firecrackers to simulate the noise of the automatic weapons they then lacked.

They had failed that time, and so many had died. Yet, in Masaya, yesterday, as we walked the streets, my friend Marco introduced me to everybody as "Richard, a writer: *he* helped us!"

Although I hadn't really been comfortable with such an introduction, it was also true that I wasn't enjoying this perfect lack of human contact either. Why had I come to La Paz today? What had I wanted?

Simply to be among the people as they went about

enjoying themselves, freely, after so many years, which was not happening for me. I was much too conspicuous everywhere I went. My Spanish wasn't good enough.

Suddenly I longed to be off those streets and out of plain sight. I could not experience their elation or their grief, their hopes, or disappointments. I stood outside them, like the spectators at the rodeo, behind my own palisades of numbness and incomprehension.

I went over to where a small huddle of people waited for the bus back to Managua, and asked when the next would be leaving.

"At five, more or less."

"And now?" I wore no watch.

The man glanced up toward the dull black glow around the sun. "It must be nearly that. To tell the truth I'm not sure."

I thought of the comandante and his wife. Would they be coming back?

The air grew muggier, and what was left of the day more overcast. I was bothered by a large fly landing on my forehead and then soaring with smutty elegance against my eyelashes.

Again and again and again it happened.

Even after I had walked a few steps farther down the road it followed me.

I began to daydream; I was in this strange and difficult place, my life threatened by a large, persistent, and lethal fly.

What should I do to protect myself in front of all these other strangers who seemed unconcerned by my plight?

I remembered an old Spanish poem:

> *Life is so beautiful*
> *it's a pity we all have to die*

Over and over I repeated the Spanish words to myself to distract myself until my bus arrived and, each time, I would reach out to grab that dangerous fly and, each time, it would go buzzing off beyond my grasp.

It was shortly thereafter that I became aware of the blaring of a loud truck or car horn.

Looking down the roadway toward Managua, I saw the tailgate of a white Toyota truck.

It was pulled off onto the shoulder of the roadway, its exhaust fluttering soft clouds of gray oily smoke.

From a window of the driver's seat a hand waved.

I ran over and leaped on and climbed the rest of the way aboard.

The only other object in the back of the vehicle was that tarpaulin, now wrapped around and around what I clearly took to be a body.

The smell was terrible: as if I had eaten death and farted it heavily out my rear end.

There were a few wreaths of colored flowers with *rojonegro* ribbons leaning against the cab of the truck.

That body seemed larger than life, swollen, as if strapped so tightly with hemp under so much tarpaulin, it had bellied out, making the tarp almost perfectly airtight, except for that escaping odor—like what is left behind after an autopsy.

Just before driving off with us in the back, my comandante friend came out of his cab and checked his tailgate again and said, "I'm sorry that you will have to ride with her cousin back to Managua. Tomorrow he will be re-buried by his *compañeros.* So if you want to come you are welcome but it just may not be pleasant for you with us."

"We're both very sorry," the wife said. "But at least you will be home before it is dark."

I thought of all the dead faces I had seen in Nicaragua, and how they were all different but the same: their final expressions a protest. Then I thought: but this corpse is probably just barely flesh and bone. I felt nauseated.

Presently, I was shivering, even though the air had gotten rather warm again and close.

After lurching forward on the left shoulder, the comandante stopped short again. "It may rain," he told me, "but you see we had no choice. The funeral is set for tomorrow in the capital when his friends will be there. If you stay on your side of the truck, and hang your head a little over the side, it should not be too bad."

With that he started up again. The wind off the corpse blew that rotten smell in my nostrils. The body was jiggling hard against the floorboards.

I decided to go upwind from the corpse and lean over the side of the truck closest to the comandante's wife.

A fresh wind blew off my face now, and after a while it began to drizzle a little, and I pushed my face out into the weather, refusing even to look back at that heap of heroic maggots opposite me.

At Mateare we passed an old bus loaded down almost to the bottom rims of its tires with passengers returning to Managua.

I banged on the side of the cab and asked to be let off.

"This isn't pleasant for us, you know," the comandante said, as I departed, "but it just had to be done."

I noticed then the absence of their little girl.

"She'll stay with my wife's family in León," he explained, when I asked, "because it wouldn't be so pleasant for her to experience a funeral such as this."

He nodded his head toward the back of the truck as we were waving goodbye.

"Go well," I called after them.

I couldn't find a place aboard the bus, and afterwards stood in that little village in the fresh air of the countryside at twilight, not worrying anymore if I would be shot by phantom paramilitaries.

Another bus would be coming along eventually. I'd wait, like all the other sad people on that Nicaraguan roadway.

Excerpt of a letter received from an American friend in Nicaragua: "I got picked up by the army at 3 a.m. Saturday (21st) and spent two hours in a becat *(jeep) racing through the night on a search and destroy mission. On one of our calls we were greeted by gunfire. Anyhow two hours later they were taking me to jail (as they said earlier they would) and we stopped off at my place for my passport. After checking out my room and suffering my outraged remarks concerning what they were doing and why, they left, without me...that's the last I've heard of that..."*

24 October, 1979

The stars over us, and the smallness of this land
but also the importance of it, of these
tiny lights of men.
—From "Lights" ("Luces") by Ernesto Cardenal
  Copyright 1979, translated by Jon Cohen

One whole night of bang-bang-bang
outside my window in Managua, darkness,
and the sound of sentries with
their weapons, and now there's no
war. But in the morning bird song
always and a great peace everywhere,
a feeling of exhaustion, as after
a death and grieving. It's not the
same everywhere in the country, I
suppose. In Diriamba, they tell me,
the soldiers have taken over everything,
and there is order, but strong dis-
approval from some quarters, and
last night, in Masaya, after dark
the town was tranquil, and the
night hid many of the scars of war
and the town seemed sleepy and
remote, a new little village at
every corner. Even the soldiers
seemed to be walking on tiptoes.
There was no other street life
because everything in town had been
destroyed, but one padded about those
empty cobbled streets like an alley
cat. M. told me people were beginning
to pay visits to each other, as a matter
of renewed sociability, but there wasn't
much anybody could offer in hospitality
except the same raw white rum. He said,
"Some people won't buy Toño beer
because they have a labor problem,
even though it's produced right here
in town."
He introduced me to a local storekeeper,
short, dark, fat, bald, with a black beret,
a "communist," in front of his shop.
"He was sent to a special party school in
Moscow," M. told me.

"Is he important?" I asked.
"He's lucky the Sandinistans don't
arrest him as a counter-revolutionary."
Then there was a loud exchange of
gunfire.
M. told me, "It happens sometimes here,
too, at night, though not as often as
in Managua. Let's have a rum, Rick."
From my September, 1979 Nicaraguan diary

Sample headline in Barricada:

BULGARIA AND THE GERMAN

DEMOCRATIC REPUBLIC SALUTE

NICARAGUAN NATIONAL DAY

Sample headline in La Prensa *that same day:*
PLURALISM GUARANTEED

"This government has been named provisionally. If we
don't do a good job you should kick us out."
—Translation of a speech by Tomas Borge, Interior
Minister, before the people of Rivas on Independence
Day.

Revolutionary Glossary

"non-Nicaraguan elements"

A euphemism for CIA who were accused of destabilizing the "revolutionary process" as in Bluefields on September 28, 1980 on the East Coast where an "undetermined number" of Black Creole-speaking Nicaraguans "demonstrated" against a heavy Cuban presence of doctors, teachers, and security agents and were jailed when riots ensued. The process of military occupation by Sandinistan militia forces from the West Coast was depicted as "reconciliation."

"Decrees #511 and 512"

Laws passed in September, 1980 by which it is "prohibited to publicize information regarding military or economic crises which might be speculative or inaccurate and thus contribute to public confusion and destabilization, creating internal security problems, without first verifying such information with the Junta of the Government of National Reconstruction." In other words, a polite expression for limited censorship of the existing press, especially the independent daily La Prensa.

"Democratic Political Future for Nicaragua"

U.S. State Departmentese for subsidizing of middle-class entrepreneurial alignments such as the Nicaraguan Coffee Growers' Association.

"anti-Cuban sentiments"

Precisely what it says, but used to depict motives other than that—i.e., counter-revolution. In fact, a good case could be made that to be pro-Cuban was to be counter-revolutionary, although this has rarely been done lately by existing political opposition groups.

"realistically"

Used to denigrate criticism, as in "the total number of persons participating realistically (in the anti-government demonstration was) ... thought to be 1000."

"La Democracia Real"

Democratic centralism without regularly scheduled elections.

"Nuestra Dignidad No Se Negocia"

We are not willing to make deals with the Western powers about domestic or external policy, but are willing to make such deals with certain totalitarian states, like Cuba, if they cannot be avoided.

"Transnational press"

Used as a term of opprobrium to describe journalists and other writers who take a critical point of view toward the New Nicaragua.

"Nuestra Revolución Es Profundamente Anti-imperialista"

True, in that the Sandinistan victory was a victory for the people of Nicaragua and, by implication, all of Central America against the smug and brutal assumptions of the rulers of the U.S. Empire who have ripped off much of Central America for centuries and imposed unpopular tyrannies, though not entirely candid, in that it takes little cognizance of other imperialisms and might be better understood as anti-Yanqui.

"El Amor Puro Incondicional Por La Patria"

Criticism, except when specifically authorized, cannot be tolerated.

"La Lucha Armada Para Arrojar A Los Invasores"

The armed struggle also, if necessary, against unpopular points of view within Nicaragua.

"Un Trabajo Arduo Y Lleno De Sacrificios"

Dealing with the possibility of discontent by recommending selflessness.

"Vende Patria"

Literally "sell out country" (middle class) as opposed to the patriotic bourgeosie (those loyal to the revolution).

II

By the Waters of Masaya

Leaving Nicaragua
(9/25/78)

Peligroso *warned the Guard,*
pointing his weapon at my heart.
Outside the war
a slower world began
beyond the speed of sound
moving above slow clouds,
a bullet, charged
with contradictory particles.
So much for dying. We drank
champagne at 30,000 feet
with the Ambassador's wife.
Her breasts were like amber,
her heart was embalmed in resins, too,
for she told me talk
of bodies rotting on the streets
in Estelí could make entertaining
the right people in Washington
this coming season difficult.
She said, you must not believe
we are all as self-absorbed and cruel
as they say we are, sucking
the moment on her amber brooch,
and then a black olive, as she
offered me her breasts and her hips
her excellent perfume and the musk
of her desire, in a handful of rebel dust.
In Washington our wheels set down
like galils *firing near the cemetery*
wall at my rebel friends in Monimbo
when I thought, by the crater lake,
by the waters of Masaya, where I sat down,
then did I cry as I remembered Zion...

Revolution

When I got back to the States after my first trip to Nicaragua in September 1978, I wrote the following in a long piece of speculative political journalism for a weekly:

"Nicaragua surprised me: a rich and fertile land, of lakes and farms, and mountains and high valleys, a warm and courteous and hospitable people. A country of poets and craftsmen. There was much that was poor and shabby and squalid, but that seemed essentially superficial, like a second growth over the potential plenty and fecundity of the countryside.

"I think we sometimes choose to believe that places like Nicaragua suffer from deficiencies of nature, in order to justify the oppressive tyrannies under which we require such peoples to live. Somehow we would like to believe they are the products of their environment; not of historic processes, but of accidents of geography, the behavior of earthquakes and volcanoes and the weather, which everybody knows nobody can do anything about..."

I would still hold with this point of view, after my second trip to the country, and I should like somehow to juxtapose the remarks with a more or less typical remark about the recent past of Nicaragua by another American writer, Paul Theroux: "...Nicaragua is the worst eyesore in the world: the hottest, the poorest, the most savagely governed, with a murderous landscape and medieval laws and disgusting food. I had hoped to verify this..."

This is the view of the informed bigot. According to his own words in *The Great Patagonian Express*, Theroux had never been to Nicaragua. He traveled all the way from Boston to Patagonia and managed to avoid the country. It was too dangerous to pass through during the revolution, he believed.

All the more reason to libel the place and its people.

If a country like Nicaragua would be a living hell under almost any government, why bother to change the government (and perhaps inconvenience the United States)?

Nearly all writings about Latin America by my countrymen attribute its miseries to faults of character and personality. During the forty-four years or more of the dynasty of the Somozas, which was installed by the U.S., the myth of hellish Nicaragua, a chronic "banana republic," developed as a corollary to the very real oppression of the Nicaraguan nation and its people.

There have been very few serious books published about Central America in our country. But looking through the library stacks on my return, I was chagrined to discover that the Nicaragua I had witnessed was not so awfully different from the Nicaragua Carleton Beals, one of the few journalists to risk his life to interview Sandino, wrote about forty years ago in *Banana Gold*.

"The credo of the Imperialist is simple:

... He never stops to try to reconcile his inner conviction that backward, dark people are incapable of progress, efficiency, honesty, or democracy with his belief that the only way for a foreign people to be happy is to be standardized into the mold already created in the United States. Because of his faith in the value of lightness of skin, he hobnobs with the aristocratic Creoles who have exploited and betrayed

their countries since the first days of independence
...Nicaragua, under our paternal tutelage for so
many years, had become the most backward and miserable of all Central American Republics."

In fact, the Somozas and their friends developed Nicaragua as their private plantation. Roads were needed to haul
produce and fight insurgencies, and they were built by
U.S. Marines. Few schools were built in the countryside.
Outside the large cities public health facilities were, at
best, primitive. The middle class which came into being
was small and resentful; eventually it became one of the
most potent insurgencies against the regime.

During the revolution, Americans still preferred to
think of Nicaragua as being essentially a sink, a sump of
subhumanity; it was that hot brutish place where we
might someday be forced to dig another canal.

My own memories of the place are probably conditioned by partisanship of a different sort. I have always
considered myself a democrat and a socialist, committed
to change, so I am uncomfortable with those who sneer at
every human effort to work towards paradise on earth.

I just don't happen to believe in original sin, and Nicaragua's problems seem capable of positive solutions.
There's enough fertile land to support its small population, and there are great riches in the soil. The people I
met seemed capable of taking matters into their own
hands, and the results produced since the revolution are
impressive: a literacy campaign has more than doubled
the number of literates; public-health and education facilities are being established in the countryside. Never having been financially supported by the CIA, I am more or
less willing to assume that Nicaraguans can utilize their
own resources to further advantage and find advantageous
means to make friendships with other nation-states on
their own terms.

The destiny of Central America is not necessarily to

become a backwater of U.S. influences. Nicaraguans and others must be free to criticize the new Nicaragua that is coming into being. However naïvely, I shall also assume that my friends are the people who have seemed friendly to me, and that the experience I have been writing about is how disorganization may lead to change.

The first time I came to Nicaragua was a time of pain and suffering. A People seemed united against a dynasty of crooks and murderers which the U.S. had supported for four decades (and which the U.S. still continues to bolster elsewhere in Central America, as, it would seem, in El Salvador).

The story of that time in Nicaragua must also be a part of the story of change:

August, 1978
(Excerpt from an article I wrote for *Geo*)

The women in bright cotton shifts, their hands across their heads, huddling thickly and plodding against each other, reminded me of the scene at daybreak only a little while ago, inside the barrio, when I had had to look at my first Nicaraguan corpse.

The people had huddled against us then to stare down at the young boy laid out with his hands by his sides in the front garden of a shack. He was all narrowed into himself, flimsy, severe, meager, like a fresh-killed doe. He had been caught in a crossfire in the dark, and nobody could say for sure if he was a genuine Sandinistan or just one of the *muchachos*.

His narrow gray face seemed untouched; only his body was shattered. Very little leakage of blood, no smell yet. All the people of the barrio gathered to look at him, whole families and gangs of street kids, and they demanded that we look, too, and take pictures. They gathered us into their huddle around his narrow form and pushed and shoved as the camera clicked, and they showed us his wounds. A pop bottle, half full, tilted next to the rib cage of this beak-faced motionless boy. It was very hot and close. Some people said there were other cadavers lying about the barrio, too, including the body of a Guardsman near the railway crossing or the drainage ditch. We looked but couldn't find anybody else killed.

That corpse stays with me, as do many others: severe, critical, not at all at peace, but ripped apart or burnt to the bone, or flayed of their souls, or grimacing with anger or chagrin. The corpses looked reproachful, like some of the living for whom they were heroes and martyrs, if that could still mean anything after so many years of so much suffering. We were always being taught what it meant to be lying dead in 1978 on a street in Nicaragua. As one man put it to me, in English, that same morning: "Don't you think your President Carter would like to see this boy?"

Other corpses came later. I think of the young man, gray as cigar ash, with a sucking chest wound. We stopped his ambulance one morning before the battle of Masaya, so the press could take photographs of his deepening torpor while his life leaked away. I think of the two Red Cross volunteers, torn to pieces by the Guard's machine guns in a clearly marked vehicle on the road out of León. At the wake, their faces and bodies in little picture-window coffins seemed to have been reassembled, in the manner of a collage, out of bits scraped off their windshield. Then I remember the odors that burning flesh gives off, so like roasting meat that the association sickens.

One morning in León, as we were huddling by a road-block next to a corpse, a thin gravel-voiced woman in black emerged from our huddle, hugging a small pot full of red beans. She pointed down with her chin toward the beans, the red beans, and said in Spanish, as though making a statement for the press, "These are the only Reds here."

... Opposite the high cemetery wall on the outskirts of León, the stillness was interrupted by the sudden clatter of machine guns. Then there was stillness again, then a couple of booms, then more stillness, and the street leading down into town was dead, flat, silent.

A Guard jeep had been scorched almost bronze. There was a smell of burning fecal matter, fetid blood. A bus was overturned, and a large new four-wheel-drive van lay on its side sprouting tulips of flame. The cupolas of the old stone cathedral glowed golden in the early morning sun. A few white flags hung from doorways. There was one *rojonegro* Sandinistan banner, and graffiti dripped on almost every wall.

A man in a green shirt stood alone in the road, skinny and bent and brown, with a bitter twisted face. "Isn't it terrible?" he said. "Isn't it such a shame?" He was for the government, he said. He had always liked Somoza and Uncle Sam, and things would have to change because "we are not all big Communists like these wise-guys in this city today..."

He stood all alone and very green in the early light, while people in their doorways called him a son of a great whore. His empty reproaches seemed to cut him off from them and us as the battle raged below. Then somebody threw a tiny firecracker that exploded near his feet. He jumped a bit and crumpled a little and sat down on the curbstone with his face against his hands.

Other people came into the gutters then with their white flags and told us how the Sandinistans had come early in the night in squads of three and five with heavy weapons, and they had organized all the *muchachos* and taken over the whole city except for police headquarters, and there had been heavy fighting through the night and even now...

Somebody pulled the string on a machine-gun far away and the bombs went "bam-bam-bam," and that sudden "whamo" with vibrato was a bazooka.

...León was still an old town of pretty pastel houses with fronts embossed with laurel, Corinthian motifs, tiles and placards, but it was being ground into dust that day. There were snipers in the ancient cathedral of Subtiava, in a barrio that was one of the principal rebel strongholds. Along the Calle Ruben Dario, near the onetime home of the great poet who led the modernist revolution in Spanish literature, was a barricade of paving stones on which the rebels had mounted a machine gun.

"A Free Homeland or Death" and "Death to the Demented Dictator" were scribbled in day-glo colors across the walls of the brand-new empty hospital where more smoking vehicles lay, but the only corpse I saw was of a mouse that looked as if it had been trampled by elephants.

The Guard's recoilless rifles went "wham-thud" and the lone Somocista got up from his curbstone and brushed himself off, as if gathering nerve from all the noise, to tell us that we would see—"they would come back, the Guard, and kill all these fucking rebel upstarts."

... Colonel Valle Salinas, chief of police of Managua, had nodded at the word "upstart" when he sat slope-shouldered like the volcano Momotombo in his small, brightly-lit office in the central jail in Managua, blowing cigar smoke at petitioners and informers alike.

The colonel had droopy, brown Pancho Villa mustaches and gold fillings. He wore gray-tinted shades, a light *guayabera* shirt, dark trousers. Over his shoulders loomed a large floor-to-ceiling photo of "El Hombre," The Man, General Anastasio Somoza Debayle, President of the Republic: debonair in a lounge suit, portly, with a Ronald Colman mustache and a shit-eating grin.

There was a double-barreled shotgun among blue-and-white flags in one corner of the room.

I said I was a journalist and asked to see some of the political prisoners. A grin froze on the colonel's face, a grin that seemed to be peelable from any outer edge, like certain decals. He sighted me between his thumbs and said, "If only there were such prisoners here, *señor*, as you think, but don't you know Nicaragua is a free country, and we don't have any political prisoners in our jails because here we have only drunks and thieves."

"And upstarts," said a lawyer in seersucker, backing his way out the door as if to curtsy.

"*Recto*," said the colonel, nodding. "*Y borrachos y ladrónes.*"

I was pushed toward the door and out into the ovenlike air of anterooms and courtyards jammed with women making inquiries about their husbands and sons...

Two Somicista portraits from my notebooks:

Renata

32, uniformed secretary in the office of a National Guard general: lives with her husband in a tiny government tract house near Tiscapa. They earn enough to own a TV, and a small Toyota. House very bare. One infant. Mother-in-law takes care.

Renata says she is not happy with the way things are for most people but "we are not the people who should be making the sacrifices."

She is thin, and paints her long nails an opalescent shade of red. Dark hair cut short.

She went to commercial school in León and found her job "through friends."

Took a holiday last year in Salvador.

Wants to go to Tampa, Florida where she has relatives.

Asked to explain her work, she says, "It's mostly all forms. I don't mind. I do it for the money, and if we have another child then maybe I'll have to stop working."

Geronimo

40, heavyset, a lawyer. One child in school in Panama. Dentistry. A son in the American school outside Managua.

Very pro-American.

Calls himself "a modernist."

"My house has all the appliances and others things you have," he says, "only here they cost so much more."

He says the extra cost is taxes as well as shipping. "Somebody has to pay to defend this country."

He claims he and his friends are bearing all the costs of this "civil war."

"The peasants have nothing and pay nothing..."

·When I mention that shack dwellers in Quinta Niña told me they paid $11 a year to the Somozas for their tiny plots of land, he replies: "Of course, they can't live there for free. We don't."

Has two small farms outside Juigalpa but claims they bring him nothing. He keeps them because they were in the family and because "the people living there must also eat."

A gold watch, a guayabera *shirt, black loafers with a high polish.*

September, 1978
(From my August-September, 1978 diaries):

Leon

An awesome quiet in the streets one goes down, and one never knows how far it's safe to go, and then the crowds, one, two, sometimes three or four people in doorways urging us to go back, take cover...

The questions from strangers and glances ("Why are you here?") and the feeling one has that one is always being watched on these streets, by one person, or another, and they are looking after you, though perhaps not always ... On the street going down toward the Guardia in León this afternoon I can't quite get the possibility out of my mind that someone might wish to shoot me, and that my only friends were all the people in the doorways...

Masaya
Soft early morning landscape with gray smoke rising above the volcanos, like shell bursts.

A Matagalpa ambulance stops us and the driver asks us about Guard roadblocks. It is racing back from Masaya with two wounded men in the back in bad shape.

Artificial plastic flower factory burning to the noise of heavy and rapid machine-gun fire, and I am reminded of a Sandinistan broadside on the burning of Managua's Frisco Disco: "Ahora Frisco Disco es Disco Frito" (Now the Frisco Disco is the Fried Disco).

National Guard resting along the sides of the highway, asleep, asprawl, like corpses.

Watching a battle from the broken window of a photographer's studio on Calle El Progresso. On the wall a photo of Miss Nicaragua in cap and gown. I watch a young Sandinistan in a baseball cap, armed with a Spanish automatic rifle, edge toward the street corner to take aim at the church steeple, but he is driven back quickly by a short burst of automatic rifle fire. The bullets kick the sides of buildings with a whap. The boy really scampers, as he falls down hard, behind some paving stones and, seeing himself still alive, smiles and turns over onto his stomach and readies his weapon again to fire.

Just Outside León

The prisoner knelt on the floor of the little wooden shed where we had been detained by two armed Guardsmen for taking photographs.

He had been hit hard many times in the face before we came into the room, and deep reddish-bluish marks stood out on his otherwise pale cheeks.

His lips were very red, as if he'd been rouged, but so were those of his frightened whimpering girlfriend: a dark plump girl in a purple blouse who stood in a corner, weeping.

He was made to turn out his pockets. Then he was asked to stand up and an officer of the National Guard felt along his calves for weapons and then undid his trousers and searched all around his privates roughly with his bare hands.

There were a couple of other Guardsmen in the room, and two plainclothes paramilitaries bearing Uzis.

The prisoner's girlfriend wept and wept. Her fear itself seemed voluptuous, the aftermath of their arrest when they had been caught necking in a place they should not have been, and were believed to be Sandinistans.

It wasn't clear to me who they were just then, but I thought they probably would be Sandinistans soon, to judge from the boy's face: narrow, angular, and pale, bruised, with one of the eyes half-closed. That face was pushed forward slightly throughout the brutal interrogation so that the slightest touch against his person registered as grave injuries to his self-esteem.

The National Guard captain who holds us at the checkpoint is friendlier than most, but today he is in a cranky mood. All this fighting means he's lost his month's vacation in September.

He tells us he has nothing against the Sandinistans. They're just another army. He would fight with them, if he thought they could win.

I say, perhaps they will win yet, because so many of the people seem to be on their side.

"The people..."

He laughs, because it's not a word he likes or feel comfortable with.

"You understand," he tells me suddenly, "I am not really political, and would serve under any government."

"Even under Commander Zero?" I ask.

"Tell me when he arrives," says the captain, before going off to help distribute rations to his men who are positioned ahead of us in a grove of trees.

How the National Guard was trained was reported by Marco Aurelio Carballo in Uno Mas Uno:

Daily in training they must attend this loud reverberating voice:
"Who are you?"
"Tigers. We are tigers . . ."
"How do tigers feed themselves?"
"With blood! Blood!"
"And from whom is this blood taken?"
"From the people. Blood of the people."

NBC cameraman viewing the marketplace in Masaya after it was bombed: "This town doesn't mean a thing anymore, having it or not having it . . ."

Photographers take pictures for the world to see of a world that must always be performing, as if for their cameras.
They are very brave, of course, and they regularly demand such access to that dangerous world that they seem, at times, when denied, like disappointed children.
The world has refused to perform again when they were present, or rather what it was performing was not the performance they really desired.

*In the San Vicente Hospital near the old cathedral of
Sutiava in León, Nicaragua, a priest shows me a spent
rocket the size of an avocado pear.*

It has American markings.

*He says, "We are none of us, safe here. We are the
enemies of this government and none of us are safe."*

*Whole families huddling against the stone floors as
ancient in their victimization and fear as when we were
slaves in Egypt.*

*The pretty, young nun who served us fried potatoes and
cold lemonade. Very little in life has ever tasted so deli-
cious. In the midst of the battle she draped a white bed-
sheet around her car and escorted us personally out of
town from the hospital, but when we got to the Centro and
saw all the troops of black berets kicking open doors and
spraying with machine guns, she was as frightened as
anybody else, and would go no further. Her fear was
contagious. We started to move but I was frozen in the
cobbled street, fearful, freaking. At first the others moved
on without me...*

*The priest from El Salvador who told me "in my coun-
try it's going to be even worse. There the heartless ones
own everything..."*

*The banker's wife who said she would prefer even the
Communists to the present regime. Learning how to bind
wounds in her barrio of Managua, she said, "It's hardest of
all on the children because they just can't go out and play
with their friends... as they might wish to..."*

*The matron who sewed a white flag on a stick so I could
walk through the streets of her city...*

*The banker who served me a Coca-Cola with ice and
said, "I am not afraid of the future. I am only frightened
now. It can't get any worse, believe me..."*

*In the hospital, a Maryknoll from Guatemala shows me
a woman giving birth. Her contractions seem to be coming with machine-gun-like rhythms, as she lies propped
on the floor above a couple of slabs of foam rubber.*

"She is in great pain," he tells me. "Yesterday she lost her sister."

The terrible smell of alcohol and rot...

In the lobby of the hotel I am approached by two whores and a pimp. For fifty dollars U.S. I can have one or both.

They say nobody is coming to see them anymore because of the fighting.

I am not interested.

Take your pick, says the pimp. My girls are hungry, but they are clean...

I go into the bar. The Minister of Tourism is sitting at a table, very drunk. He waves me over. He claims he saw me at General Allegrette's funeral.

A slight tone of menace to every invitation; his face is pale and puffy. He wears a kind of sailor suit: white tunic and sky-blue kerchief. It's the National Day. I'd forgotten. He tells me he is very worried about his children at home in his finca. He's never been separated from them overnight. He asks, "You got any children?"

When I tell him yes, he asks, "Why did you come to Nicaragua, anyway?"

We speak in Spanish because his English is thickened by alcohol beyond comprehension. He tells me he speaks no other languages. He is Minister of Tourism and, before that, was Minister of Labor.

"Have you ever worked with your hands?" I ask.

"Never."

The next morning, early, left for Rivas. On the road south, we pick up a school teacher from Juigalpa. He is going to see relatives in Granada. He says, "It would be better for you if I went the rest of the way alone;" we leave him on the road beyond Masaya.

Stopover in San Juan Del Sur. Beautiful cove beach and

warm water. Boys playing soccer on the sand. Fishing boats. A Victorian frame house: HQ of the Somocista Youth Organization. Big sign on the beach, a billboard in blue and white:

SOMOZA FOREVER

Driving back up from the beach, a man on a horse comes alongside us and announces, "Someday..."
We can't hear the rest, and drive past.
I am reminded of Sanchez from La Prensa *who always is full of ominous forebodings. Said to be a Sandinistan theorist. Speaks in heavily abstracted Spanish. I get every other word.*

Soldier looking at my safe-conducts: "This doesn't say the way you think. It tells me who you are..."
Woman reporter at Nica Press Society offices near Banana Bar: "We haven't any time to lose. You must know everything and you are way behind."
Colonel Aranda, when I asked to borrow a copy of Old Somoza's book on Sandino: "We'll see..."
As if he had a favor to bestow...
The smell of rotten cheese and dung in the lean-to when we stop for lunch.
The woman in the store in Rivas near the Guard cuartel selling me a pint can of Kern County Tomato Juice: fourteen cordobas, more than a dollar...
The paintings of barrio life in the banker's house: thatch huts, mud streets, pigs, bright colors, and young boys with automatic rifles...
Breaking my glasses in Masaya during the fighting, I could see distance but was unable to see precisely what I was scribbling on every page.

A helpless feeling on cobble stones, with my sandles slapping so that I trip when I run.

The saddle maker in Caterina near Masaya has either died or run away.

Blood all over the floors of the empty shell that was his house.

I came to ask him to make something for my daughter.

The neighbors don't know what has happened, or they won't say.

The woman at the juice bar says, "He's not the only one."

She's from Acuahalinca "where there are footsteps in the mud a million years old."

"Not so old."

"Old enough."

Conversation with a boy in a baseball cap: "Would you fight?"

"How do you know I don't?"

The chief man in Quinta Niña leading us around the barrio. We pass an open doorway where a young man is cleaning a silver pistol.

"I hope you did not see that," he tells me. "Let me show you where we bathe."

He leads us down toward the filthy lake where some concrete tubs have been set into the soil to catch rainwater.

The women do laundry there, too.

Driving through Masatepe, my companion tells me "both the Sandinos and the Somozas came from around here."

At the U.S. Ambassador's briefing everything is off the record except for a prepared statement read by the Ambassador deploring the violence.

The press becomes impatient: will the Ambassador comment on certain specific atrocities of the regime?

Through channels, off the record, we are told that demarches *have been made.*

Has the U.S. made contact with the Sandinistas?
No comment.

There are maybe twenty of us in attendance, in addition to the Ambassador, a few marine guards, and a man who is identified as Mr. Martin.

We're told we can't take Mr. Martin's picture or record his voice, but he will answer further questions.

Have the Sandinistas been in touch with U.S. officials?

"You could say we are speaking to every interested party in order to reach a peaceful solution, etc., etc., etc...."

The Ambassador is a former academic of Spanish descent.

The taxi driver who brings me back from the briefing says the U.S. has no friends left in Nicaragua.

At the hotel, Mr. Martin again, with a group of Peace Corps volunteers who have been brought in from the countryside for evacuation.

I go over to where he's sitting to ask something about the Ambassador. How long has he been in Nicaragua?

"Ask the Ambassador," he says. "You don't really want to know anyway...I'm busy."

September 10

Martial Law has been declared and we must take our copy to the National Guard for pre-censorship, according to Guard Communiqué #53 from the offices of Colonel Achilles Aranda Escobar.

In the offices of the National Guard are piles of brand new copies of old man Somoza's story of why he had to murder Sandino, "The Truth About Sandino," with a bloody dagger on every cover. In an adjacent office a colonel with a gun on his hip, who speaks no English, says he cannot pass on what I have written until it has been translated into Spanish, but now that I get the general drift of the way things are being run at their headquarters, I go back to my room and call San Francisco collect and read what I have written over the air, live, on KPFA-FM accompanied by the sounds of gunfire well beyond our hotel windows.

La Paz Centro

The little village called La Paz Centro in September 1978 was a small dusty place of rutted lanes, a white church, a Guard *cuartel* with a sand-bagged veranda-style porch, and lots of shabby grocery stores. You couldn't see much of it from the roadway going to León. It was in about three hundred yards from the road. The highway bore only a road marker, a pottery stand with a backyard kiln, and a couple of thatch-roofed restaurants where they sold *carne asado, tacos,* and *cacao.*

Coming and going from the great battles, I sometimes stopped to eat or for a *refresco.* Under the thatch, in the cool air, among the good smells of the food, was another easier world. Nobody ever talked about the war or about politics. If they knew where you had just been or were going to, the handsome woman and her daughters and her old man might nod with a certain knowingness. But they always went right to work filling your belly as fast and as well as they could. They made you sit at one of their tables and they offered you a Ron or a Cerveza, if they thought you looked at all pained.

I had been taught by a friend to drink the *cacao* which is made of a ground-up chocolate powder and maize. It's served cool and sweet, scented with a nuttiness, and served in pretty round-bottomed wooden gourds, scratched out with decorations, that are made to rest on little coasters so they won't wobble.

The people who owned the place were at least part Indian; and they hadn't served too many gringos much aside from certain bottled drinks or maybe cigarettes or rum, so they seemed pleased with my lack of squeamishness. If, despite the flies, I was willing to risk my stomach on rice and beans and one of their own *refrescas*, that seemed flattering to them. They got to know all of us after a while, and they called us by various names: *"La Señora Rubia," "El Alto," "El Señor Gasiosa."* Always in good fun.

I'm not even sure they knew we were journalists.

The morning after León fell to the Guard I stopped there on the way back from looking at corpses roasting on the streets, which was done as a sanitary precaution; and I had no appetite. It would be another hour before I would get back to Managua. I felt I should take something. But, earlier, in the marketplace of the old city, I has been badly frightened when a Guard patrol came around a corner at me firing into the air to scare off looters.

I guess I was just depressed and hot and unhappy with myself for not doing more, as if what I did finally mattered, saved lives, won victories, changed the face of Nicaragua. Being a member of the press and watching defeats come about because of the overwhelming arms the U.S. had once supplied to the Somozas, it made me angry, with nobody to blame. The people were willing to die. But I was not.

That morning the patron of La Casa Tropica was toting a double-barreled shotgun in front of the food counter under his thatch-roofed hut; and I noticed another of the hangers-on wearing a sidearm. None of his women seemed about the place, behind the counter or in the cooking shed open to the air next door. A large scraggly old rooster pecked at the dirt floor. A dog was snoring at the patron's feet. Sitting all by himself at a corner table, a businessman from Managua in a suit and tie ate rice and beans and sipped from a Cerveza.

The patron greeted me, "*¿Que quieres?*"

I ordered a *cacao*.

"I can't serve you that," he told me in Spanish, with a shrug.

"You didn't make any?"

"It was impossible," he explained. "The women are afraid to go to the marketplace."

"Is that why you are armed?"

"Everybody stays inside," he said. "There are rumors of all kinds. The Guard is castrating young men, they say. Terrible rumors..."

"Do you think it's true?"

He didn't answer and I was sorry for my question. With so much bloodshed and terror everywhere, why should his fears seem irrational?

I said I would have any bottled drink or *refresca*.

He showed me all his yellow teeth: "No have, you know. There is really very little..."

"I'm sorry to ask."

"*Hijo putas,*" (sons of bitches) said the patron.

I had started back away from the counter toward the roadway where my car was parked, when the man from Managua dropped his fork, and said in that careful English, which is often a gesture of timorous friendliness, "He is ashamed, you know, to offer his rice and beans, and it will not do for you to take his lemonade."

"I would take his lemonade. He need not be ashamed."

I had been on a special medication all the time in Nicaragua and had no stomach problems—the source of my culinary bravery.

The man from Managua started to tell the patron that I was very thirsty, but he insisted he could not serve me anything. It was impossible. It would not be good for me. And there was so very little left for the others.

I felt he was saying he would offer nothing to this *gringo*—after León—and it was hurtful to me.

I got back inside my rented car and started the engine. I wouldn't try another place. I'd wait until I was back in Managua.

The car lurched forward. Through the rear-view mirror I looked for a pause in the oncoming traffic so that I could get on the highway, and in the mirror saw a young man from the village in a little shed behind a neighboring house washing out some clothes in a galvanized metal bucket.

Then I looked again and saw it was a short-haired woman in jeans. She wore a baseball cap and had dark Indian skin, and she seemed very pleased when I waved to her.

The patron came up to the window of my car with his shotgun; he also had with him a frosty bottle of Pepsi, and he passed it through the window and insisted he would take no money.

"Here there is no custom for this," he explained. "It is not in favor. Here in La Paz..."

Before I could say a word, he added: "Also we hate the *tanketas Norte Americanos...*"

"The armored cars are British," I explained. "Only the larger Sherman tanks are American."

"And the rifles? And the rockets? The machine guns..."

"Yankee or, in some cases, Israeli."

"Indeed." He gave me a meaningful glance.

"The Somozas also," I quipped.

"Made in the States," he said with a smirk.

"*Tardes...*"

"*Suerte...*"

The bottle felt cold against the insides of my thighs as I gunned the motor.

"God damn son of a bitch fucking bastards," said the patron, in English, too.

It wasn't said at me, but was a statement to the air—to which I was asked to give assent.

I spat out the Spanish word for cowards.

"Cocky sucky sons of bitches," repeated the patron.

Some Pepsi fizzed up from the open bottle and dribbled across my lap.

"I could get you a rag," said the patron.

"It's not necessary," I said, "many thanks," and drove away.

In Managua I was thirsty again as soon as I walked into the air-conditioned lobby of my hotel, and I bought a round of drinks for all my friends in the bar, including, alas, a couple of Central Americans who may have been government spies.

A Dream:
"Cocktails at Somoza's"

Somoza was holding a cocktail party "at home" in his estranged wife's private ranch-style mansion, El Retiro, in Managua, for the press. The Dictator had left his "bomb proof" bunker to be at this event. His son was there and his half-brother and his PR man, Wolfson, and some generals and a few attractive women, some of whom may have been available, but not his mistress, Dinora. This was Tacho, the family man, on view. There was every kind of drink you could want from a set-up bar in the main hall. A waiter in a red monkey jacket passed around a silver tray of cocktail franks in "blankets."

Because of his bad heart, the Dictator was only taking mineral water. He had on his nicest Kolmer-Marcus-type lounge suit and black Italian loafers with tassels. A white-on-white shirt, a benevolent smile for everybody who took a drink or ate a frank or a little *schmear* of chopped liver on a piece of rye crisp.

"Enjoy yourselves," he told us all: "It's my party."

There were very few bodyguards in evidence; the waiters all wore pieces. My invitation said "cocktails at four." The accordionist played "Managua, Nicaragua is a Wonderful Town," and "*Arrivederchi Roma.*"

"I could probably get you some really good shit from

Panama," said a fellow from the Exterior Ministry, Scala-mandre. "Also some Colombian blow. No problems..."

The Ambassador to the World Bank and his wife were introduced. She had very soft hips, long legs, nice full breasts, a blasé fuckable air. But I was with a Lanica stewardess who doubled as an "agent in place" for U.S. special envoy Bowdler.

"Keep your eyes to yourself," she told me.

Nobody would introduce me to the gray-haired man in the shiny black moleskin suit who kept finger popping to the music.

A waiter came by with a platter of gefilte-fish balls and dip.

We talked about torture.

The Dictator walked past, patted me on the shoulder, and asked, with a big grin, if I was "having a good time."

Tachito entered with a pretty Dutch photographer.

Dan Rather of CBS was jiving one of the hostesses, and old George Nathanson of CBS Radio was blithering to the Agricultural Minister, Klaus Singeleman, about the decline of the dollar in Argentina.

The man from *Readers Digest* said, "Now this is what I call a civilized party..."

The stewardess asked me if I would like to take her home.

She said she had been close to Henry Kissinger in the old days in New York. Did I know Henry Kissinger?

"I never even made it with Midge Decter," I explained.

She said, "People say I look like Joan Collins, the actress..."

"I think you look like Barbara Walters on the TV," I said. "But maybe it's all these journalists...the atmosphere..."

"You should stay a while," said Somoza. "We'll have supper. You like fish? Meat? Anything you like. I got a real good cook. You ought to try his *fettuccine alfredo* with black-bean sauce..."

Words to that effect...

He told us last time he was in Miami he had bought the most expensive Cuisinart food processor for the *minceur* and a great big Sony Trinitron. We could watch a football game later on a cassette? Maybe Southern Cal, or Penn State, whichever I liked, and then maybe "All in the Family."

The girl from Pan Am told me she had once "dated" Eden Pastora, Commander Zero, presently Deputy Minister of the Interior under Tomas Borge. "Did you know he drives a brand new Caddy Seville?" she told me.

"I wouldn't be surprised . . . "

"He doesn't really like women," said Somoza. "None of the rebels do. They treat women just like objects."

He laughed, and the girl was nodding: "Tacho is a very sensitive person. He knows how to be nice to a woman. Show a girl a good time."

Somoza said, "You should stay in Nicaragua if you like women. We got some real nice beauties here . . . Bianca Jagger was nothing . . . "

He was sitting on a big "sectional" sofa with his legs apart, two-handing a large frosty glass of mineral water.

"If you ask me," said Somoza, "the only place to stay in Miami is Cocoanut Grove or the Key Biscayne Yacht Club. I don't go for all that flashy stuff along the beach in my condition."

I complimented him on the cut of his suit.

"I'll introduce you to my tailor," said Somoza. "You'd be surprised how reasonable he is if you order in quantities . . . "

The man from the Chicago Tribune was talking bridge with a diplomat from El Salvador.

Somoza said, "You can get whatever you like in Nicaragua and really have a good time. Just be a regular fella, will you?"

"War is a bad business," Somoza said: "Believe me I don't like it any better than you do."

He said, "I can be a nice guy, a regular fella. Just try me . . . "

Somoza said, "Honestly, Dickel, you don't know what I have to put up with sometimes. It makes my blood boil."

"I don't think I'd like to be around when that happens," said my date.

"Have another drink Dicky boy...A tidbit...maybe some shrimp with pineapple," said Somoza. "You like a good steak? I bet you'd like a really good steak."

Outside the mansion, the sidewalks of Managua were all empty. The streets were deserted. Even the barricades looked abandoned; there weren't any soldiers about.

"He's a good host," said my date. "He'd do anything to please his guests."

"Except resign. Too bad about his ticker," I added.

"I grant you," she said, "he isn't as active as he used to be, but he still carries on. He's done it all for Tachito's sake. He really loves that boy."

"I could tell," I said.

She said, "I admire a good family man. Don't you?"

"Not that I'm aware of," I said.

"You ought to get to know him a little better," she said. "You'd like him. He's very cordial and businesslike. A real swinger. Pretty regular guy..."

"I don't like the smell of his after shave," I said.

"At least make the effort," she told me.

"It's hard to get too close to anybody who uses so much heavy after shave."

"Try," she said, "make the effort."

"Have another drink," I said. "A little piece of gefilte fish..."

"How about some nookie?" she asked me.

I asked her if she knew of a good Chinese restaurant in Managua, and she told me there was a brand new one right around the corner from the National Guard hospital called The Golden Dragon.

The Tipitapa Baths

In Tipitapa, half an hour from Managua, there's a "model prison." The signs on the road point you to it, but you can't go inside. You can just see the walls. In the old days, a brother of the present Somoza built the place, I was told, and many Nicaraguans used to say it was exemplary because "you went inside a prisoner and when you came out you were a cadaver." Now the prisoners are all fairly low-ranking former National Guardsmen, and there have been no reports of recriminations against them taking place there.

Near the prison sign the highway forks. If you went to the left you'd go through town, around the barricaded Guard *cuartel* and out the other end to some sulphur baths that were once fairly popular with the better classes from Managua. (It was in Tipitapa a long time ago that the U.S. Marines forced a peace treaty on the Liberal Moncada who was in revolt against the old Conservative government.)

It's not a very large place. There's an outdoor dining pavilion and dance floor; a low U-shaped building with motel-style units where people from the city can stay overnight or for weekends; and two rectangular concrete hot pools, below, along a terraced hillside that overlooks a cow pasture, a gorge, and a wrecked steel bridge on which is mounted a red pennant with just one word: *Peligroso*.

Dangerous! The whole place was enclosed by ornamental iron gates which were bent out of commission some years back when a truck missed a curve in the narrow two-lane highway and came sailing up the front lawn of the spa. All the buildings beyond these unworkable gates were an ugly pistachio-green stucco roofed with dark orange tiles.

Inside the dance pavilion there was a large juke box decorated with colored lights. Many tables surrounded the dance space. There was a bar and a snack bar, Coca-Cola signs, and ads for Ron Flor De Cana, and Victoria Cerveza.

After the fighting began, hardly any Managuans took the trip to Tipitapa. The local people, when they came to use the baths, brought their own frayed towels and carried food with them in little paper bags.

The place wore its emptiness without abandon. Everything seemed pretty much in order except the pistachio walls were all cracking and peeling; lawns thick with dead leaves. Like with too much of Nicaragua's volcanic terrain, you had the feeling, as you walked across those soft grassy lawns, that your foot might suddenly sink deep into the soil and release a huge jet-like effusion of steam or lava.

Tipitapa is a market town surrounded by large *fincas* producing cotton, the country's principal cash crop. Like "Open Tres" and other outlying wastelands, it swelled at the time of the great earthquake of 1973 with some of Managua's battered surplus population. Some textile mills opened nearby, a pottery, and a few other small factories owned by a family of Miami sharks named Gorn. On the day I visited, a general strike had been on for three weeks; in town, grown men played pool and wagered, sullenly; the market women haggled with each other.

At the baths a couple of local teenagers played splash games in the farthest pool; in the steamy vaporous air their faces seemed all awobble.

Another dark little boy in rags was their attendant. He

busied himself with a shovel and push broom making a huge pile of hot green mud.

The near pool was entirely deserted. It looked as if nobody had been dunking in it in quite some time, but it had not been emptied out: dead leaves floated on its steamy surface. I bent low over the water and there was a reek like dead fish or blood.

The patroness, a European woman, did not wish to talk about what had become of all of her customers.

She claimed she was too busy.

Besides, she averred, they still came, "some of them," on the weekends. "It's true, *señor*."

But when I asked if I might drop in over the weekend to have another look around, she said she did not think people would like to be disturbed when they came to her spa, though she could not stop me.

She said her customers liked privacy.

"Some of the men do not bring their wives," as if to put a certain spice into her baths for me.

"*Entiendo*."

"I *spik* English," she said.

She seemed to wish me to go now because she had so much to do, but it was hot and muggy, too uncomfortable to rush anywhere.

I asked if there was any Coke or coffee to be had at her snack bar. "Not today," she said. "For the weekend only. When it's like this," she shrugged, "I do not prepare."

"Why don't the people come anymore?" I asked.

"It's a very old place this place here."

She shrugged again.

"So?"

"It was once much better. Now we do not have the money."

She was small and leathery-faced and brown-haired. She may have once been attractive; now her face with its large pores looked as if it had been tanned in too much sulphurous water and vapor. Her eyes were dull, without any particular focus.

Sometimes she seemed to be inspecting a crack in the bathhouse wall over my shoulder. At other times she was talking to the ground or to that large dark shady almond tree near the front gate.

Never directly at me.

"You see," I told her then, "I thought it must have something to do with the Sandinistans..."

"*¿Que?*"

She knew the word as well as I did. "*Los Rebeldes*," I explained.

"It has nothing to do with any such things like that," she told me, loudly, in Spanish.

"Not with the shooting?"

"Where do you hear shooting?" Her voice was accusatory: "We have no war here. There is no war. There were just some disturbances, and many of my customers who are with the army or the police they know that and they tell me it will soon be over because they are with the government."

"*Claro.*" I felt disappointed with her for pretending to be hopeful. Very few people in Nicaragua were doing so at that point.

From the terraced hill I heard a barrage of splashing and the hilarity of the young bathers.

She held her ground and smiled at me, almost lubriciously: "Now do you wish to bath here?"

I shook my head "no" slowly.

"It is just the same with us," she said. "It does not matter."

As if responding to an insult.

As she showed me toward the front gate, I pointed at the ruined bridge.

It had been splintered right through its central span, as if by heavy axe blows: Trusses, metal beams, and girders seemed bent, warped, twisted. There was a gaping hole in the roadway.

Three young men balanced their way along the girders with their arms outstretched, and when they came to the hole they bent down and looked into the gorge and backed away again.

"I am sure that happened with the *terremoto*," I lied, deliberately making sure to use the Spanish word for earthquake so I would be understood.

"*Sí*," she said. "Earthquake... *de algodón con la dinamita... claro...*"

"*Es lástima*," I said. "*Peligroso...*"

"*Claro, Peligroso*," she said, as if admitting to a crime, and then she put a finger to her lips and repeated the word, loudly and slowly: *Peligroso*."

More like a warning to me, as I turned and went out through her gates.

Irwin

Irwin stood inside one of the glass public booths at the crowded noisy airport telephone exchange in Managua and called his "one good friend" in the States "person to person, collect," in California.

"Phil? It's Irwin here. Hey. Long time no speak, big buddy. Where am I? Phil, you accepted the charges so you know I'm in Managua, just like always, only I gotta get the hell out of here.

"I'm caught right in the middle of it. Thanks, buddy. Knew I could count on ya."

As he listened to his long-distance friend go on and on, Irwin's forehead grew very wet, and his grin froze on him.

"Gold? What gold?" Irwin suddenly demanded. "I could never get near any...Sure there's gold down here but I never got near any. It's all Somoza's, you dig. Honest I swear..."

Abruptly his whole face fell. "You mean you can't really help?" His jaw seemed to be disintegrating; there were hollows in his cheeks.

Irwin said, "If I stick around they'll kill me. Honest, old buddy, either one side or the other. Sure I'll wait...You'll call me right back?"

He rattled off the number for the airport telephone exchange and then demanded: "Be sure to call me back now, you hear."

And when he hung up Irwin saw me and recognized me from the Hotel Intercontinental lobby, and he seemed just very sheepish-looking.

"Trouble?" I asked.

"My only good friend in the world," Irwin declared, "and even he won't help out. Because he says he can't."

"...some fucking world," went Irwin. "He wanted me to come down here so we both could get rich and now..."

He said no more, as if stuck, lodged against a clot of solid lucid rage.

I asked Irwin what he planned to do next.

"He's gonna call me back. Said he would. I'll wait and see."

But Irwin didn't wholly believe his friend. He mopped at his tall bald domed head with a colored kerchief and cursed silently.

On the crown of that large head were many depressions, dents, little scars. Irwin looked as if he had never done anything much except been battered about by life. He had big cry-baby eyes and a nasal whine.

We sat down to take some coffee together at the airport café and I asked where he was from.

"Near the Bronx."

"Where exactly?"

"The Bronx," he corrected himself, swallowing hard: "Just off the Grand Concourse. Grant Avenue."

"I've been there."

"It's mostly all savages now," Irwin said.

"Do you really think so? I don't think so."

"Honestly," he shook his head at me, "I don't want to die down here..."

"What were you doing here?" I asked. "Why did you come?"

"You heard." He shrugged with discouragement. "For once in my life I thought I'd get a little bit ahead of the game. Gold," went Irwin, "shit, there's plenty of gold here all right but no way to get at it unless you've got your own private army, like the Somozas. It's all swamps and mountains down there, rain forests," he said, with a malarial shiver, "and full of savages, Somoza people, multinational types. On the Rama River I almost got shot more than once."

"And now?"

"What do you think? I'm broke."

"And my only friend in the world who stakes me here wants me to just stick it out come hell or high water. Shit," Irwin said. "It doesn't seem fair. He's in advertising in LA. That's a safe business. But down here..."

I asked, "How much do you think you would need to get by?"

"It isn't that," Irwin shook his head again, "I probably have enough to get back home, but if I go back empty-handed they will probably kill me."

"Nice friends."

"He has partners. He's the only good friend I ever had. I never had any other."

Irwin got up wearily from the table and went slouching off toward the counter to bug the woman about his incoming call.

I followed.

A large class of neatly-jacketed blond Mormon school-boys stood in a bunch near the TACA Airlines counter, and when I passed, one asked if I was an American, and when I said I *was* they all said they were Latter-Day Saints and they were flying home on the next flight out to the States because there'd been fighting near their school in the hills above Managua.

I told them I thought that was interesting, but I had to find my friend at the telephone exchange.

Then a boy with pimples told me, "The Nicas are all leaving, just like us. It's going to be a revolution. They say Castro is behind it."

"Or in front," I said, waving to Irwin through a milling mob.

At the telephone exchange I asked him, "Why not leave and go someplace else? Like Florida... until your friend cools out."

"I never really like to admit defeat," Irwin said.

"It wasn't really your fault."

"He's my only goddamn friend in the world," Irwin said. "He'll find me sooner or later."

"How?"

"My goddamn mother would tell him. You know the way things are. She thinks more of him than of me."

"Why is that?"

"Because he's smart. He gets other people to do his business for him. My friend never risks his own life."

"Irwin, is that you talking or your mother?"

"My mother didn't want me to go down here," he said. "But if I was gonna go I shoulda come back rich."

"So you went."

"And I got nothing to show for it."

His mouth tightened on him.

He wiped at his long domed head.

The woman at the counter glanced up and said she had a call for Irwin Goldberger from San Luis Obispo, California, in Cabinet 3.

Inside the glass booth, Irwin shouted "Hello" very loudly and nasally into the phone, as if he really were trying to reach across a long distance, and then he shouted it again: "Hello."

Nobody seemed to be answering.

I started to walk away.

A woman in a pants suit stopped me to ask if I had any dollars to give her for cordobas.

I didn't.

Irwin gesticulated frantically at his long-distance friend from his little glass booth.

I came closer.

Irwin said, "Don't give me Bluefields. There's nothing in Bluefields but savages..."

"...I already told ya," he said, "it's a civil war, a revolution. Can I help that?"

"Hey don't talk to me like that," Irwin said. "You're my buddy, my friend."

"Hey," Irwin said, "don't please..."

He said, "Aw what the hell. If I could I would..."

"You're nuts," he said, "crazy..."

He said, "Please don't say things like that to me. I tried. Honest..."

A shrapnel of words. Wheedling. Cajoling.

"I told ya goddammit there's a war on here...and I don't wanna get myself killed..."

"Aw, don't be that way..."

As I left I had the feeling that if the Sandinistans came marching into Managua, as they eventually did, Irwin would still be haggling over the long-distance phone with his friend about the gold he had never found along the banks of the Rama River.

And he would probably never go looking for that gold again, because it was too dangerous, he had too many excuses, and he no longer had a friend in the world to back him.

Fabrizio and the Captain

At the entrada to the town of Jinotepe I saw Fabrizio, "the half-wit," pumping away at his small chrome two-wheeler bike up the main avenue. A detachment of *guardia*, on foot, were also moving up the main avenue.

Fabrizio grinned at them just like a half-wit as he pedaled past.

He was eighteen years old and his real name was Roberto. He came from the Indian barrio of Masaya, from an artisan family. In Jinotepe he served as lookout and messenger, passing himself off as one of the locals.

Big in the shoulders, he had rather short legs, a wide brown face which he could distort in bicycling to resemble a grotesque Mayan mask. The Guard always mocked him as a "defective." He had a very subtle set of signals for his friends: when he was wearing his baseball cap it meant one thing, when he was without it it meant another. He'd once explained his signals to us, but I had forgotten which was which. As a member of the press, I preferred not to be too involved in such machinations.

This afternoon he was bareheaded, and seemed to be pedaling toward the very place I was standing, alongside Captain Arguello beneath the dark spread of a large almond tree.

The day was warm, bright, unusual weather for the rainy season. Arguello had set up his operating post beneath the tree in order to frisk suspicious persons leaving and entering the city.

Among members of the press, Arguello was known as Mr. Nice Guy. He called himself a professional, more like a cop than a soldier, and claimed he wanted to study penology at the University of California in Berkeley, once the present "disturbance" was put down.

He was a dapper young man of no more than thirty, neatly turned out in his blousant camouflage fatigues which he'd had specially tailored. Soft spoken, not the usual sort of bully, he'd trained in the Canal Zone, like most of the others, but said he didn't like "warfare." Still there had been massacres in Jinotepe, as in all the other towns, including the murder of four young students in the marketplace only weeks ago. I'd seen the placard of metal the market people had fastened to a building wall commemorating that event.

Arguello was still a bachelor. He hoped to remain so a while longer. He said once you get married a man must either lie all the time or stop living. His mother and brother owned a small coffee *finca* in the hills near Masatepe, the area where the Somozas and the Sandinos had originated. He said his brother had married but also kept an Indian concubine. They'd had three children together, and her husband worked as his overseer, a hopeless incompetent, kept on only because of his wife. He said so many of the Indians were like that.

"You know me," he said in his rubbery Spanglais, "I believe in modern ways, but if we lose the *finca* we will have nothing else, ever I think."

"Why did you become a soldier?" I asked.

"To avoid half-wits like that one over there," he told me and nodded toward Fabrizio who was now criss-crossing unsteadily along the cobbled square on his bike.

"In the countryside," he went on, "people have nothing, and this is the way they come out. They're like this one, or they die. It's a perversion of real life, you know."

I had to seem to be in agreement, not wishing to seem too argumentative and cause Arguello to notice me with other than his general air of indifference and contempt. But I was also thinking about very mundane and practical and "modern" things such as health care, running water, schools... Could they possibly alter the perversions he seemed to think were so general?

He seemed to anticipate my thoughts because he said, "Every day I watch that one and he's just like my country in general... so backward... pushing himself nowhere on his little kid's bicycle... If he and his kind run the world, Somoza and his friends will not seem so bad after all..."

"You think so."

He laughed, like a chest cough: "I'm no philosopher...I think so... yes. Why would I say this to you otherwise?"

He seemed cross with me, and removed a pack of Luckies from the specially-fitted pocket in the sleeve of his tunic and offered one to me.

I refused because they were much too strong, and I had been smoking more than I should have.

He coughed again, like a laugh: "You probably prefer marijuana?"

"Not while I'm here in Nicaragua," I insisted, and removed my pack of Marlboro filter tips and offered one to him.

He removed three cigarettes and placed them in the breast pocket of his tunic and lit up a Lucky. When he said thanks he blew out a dollop of acrid white smoke as if we were witnessing a very frosty afternoon together.

Just at that moment, to my alarm, Fabrizio stopped his bike a few yards from where we were standing, and dismounted, letting the bike fall with a clatter.

"What can I do for you?" asked the Captain, as he approached.

Fabrizio grinned, all teeth: "Nothing."

Arguello seemed unable to accept such an answer: "Nothing? Why did you stop? Do you think this journalist will take your picture, and they will send for you in Hollywood?"

"There really was no reason," Fabrizio replied, his voice thick with phlegm: "No harm meant...I was tired so I stopped..."

"He stopped!" Arguello shrugged at me, as if to indicate the extent of the mess he had to deal with every day. "So go now," he added. "This is a military OP. You must not loiter...even you, Don what-did-you-say-your-name-was?"

"Half-wit," Fabrizio grinned: "Agreed. I'll go now. Sorry." He seemed so very humble and scraping. No trouble there. "Good day, Yankee."

He grinned at me.

"Good," I waved back.

Fabrizio stumbled as he backed away from us toward his bicycle.

When he pedaled away, around the corner and out of sight, the Captain said: "People like that...country people...do you want them to be your friends?"

"I really don't know such people well," I said. "It's never been possible for me to know such people."

"Well I do."

Arguello took a clip from his bandolier, which he wore across his chest, and slammed it into the stock of his Uzi, and with his finger released the safety.

When he looked at me again, his face was very stern and the gun was pointed obliquely at my chest.

I must have given him all the wrong answers because the captain recommended that I get inside my car and immediately drive back to Managua or he would not be sorry.

"Thanks very much..."

As I moved out through the *entrada* I heard a distant spattering of small-arms fire.

The Battle of Masaya

(An Eye-Witness Account, by Ramon)

"All during the battle of Masaya my friend was around the corner in his house, only three blocks away. Maybe one hundred meters. Less. He was in his house with his wife and kids, I thought, when I was in the fire station on the floor, like a cadaver. I thought they would be safe here, too, though I could not go to his place. The Guard controlled the intersection; they did not respect the white flag. The Sandinistans were firing down from the church steeple in Monimbo. It was a flood.

"All during the battle I thought about my friend, and it was just a lot of big noise and scariness where I was, safe on the floor next to the tile walls. I waited until the planes had come and gone three times; I waited even after the water trucks came. Then I went over to see my friend.

"The Guard was patroling the business district to protect us from looters. Some people had broken into Somoza's bank; they said they would shoot anybody who looted, but the people were hungry, and the only things they could find in the looting and the cinders were bottles of *aguadiente* and Ron Flor.

"People were getting drunk, and I don't blame them. The whole town was a mess. The cars on the *esquinas* were all scorched. Overturned. There was a boy with half his face blown off near the Donald Duck Snack Bar. I didn't have to look to know he was dead.

"Just a lot of blood on the walls. Some people made marks in green where soldiers died. Crosses inside circles. I counted six, maybe ten, in Monimbo alone.

"Near the saddlemaker's house a man stood on the road with a big chunk of dog meat. His hands were all bloody. He offered to sell me this meat for my family. He said it was 'heart.' We don't like no heart. Then he said it was 'the heart of General Blessing,' and he was crying: *Hijo De La Puta...Hijo De La Puta...*

"At my friend's house they told me look for my friend in the old marketplace and there it was all burned out and they said he took his family and they were on their way south to Rivas.

"I asked about his wife and children from some neighbors and they said sure they were in Granada, but I didn't think so because the house was not boarded up like that. It seemed they could not be away for very long.

"I went back to the fire station thinking I would also check for him at the main Red Cross, if he was there or people knew of his welfare, but I was stopped by the main Guard patrol.

"This soldier he was drunk on *aguadiente*, just like a looter, and he waved a bottle at me. I should come with him across the way to the park where some others sat in a Becat. They were shooting rifles into the air to scare all the looters.

"The noise was very frightening and I thought they would point those things at me.

"They took away my Kodak Instamatic camera and they said I should not be taking pictures because this place would be like a scar on Nicaragua forever.

"So they took away my camera my friend had given me when we were in the camera club together, and they just pretended to throw it away into this pile of burning rubbish and stuff. But I knew they would take it for their own.

"Then they said I must come with them to be questioned and they made me go with them to the Guard *cuartel* to see General Nemesis behind the barricade, and there I saw my friend's body in front of an earthmoving machine.

"These two orange Becats had been burned good, and there was also a whole pile of rebel bodies, too, and I only recognized it was Rudolfo because he was wearing the yellow sweater we gave him for the anniversary of his licentiate.

"It was a pretty hot day and his body had started to get big like a pie crust. Underneath the yellow sweater he lay face down next to a dead woman. I could not see their faces.

"There was just a little smell and some flies. I smelled a lot worse things in the fish wharves at Corinto.

"Well I saw no dead Guardsmen. Just my friend. He was dead, and this woman I didn't know, and a couple of young boys.

"The Sergeant said the Red Cross would come and burn them. They were waiting so there would be no more looters.

"Nothing much I could do there so I thought I should go find his wife and tell her the bad news. The Guard said I must not leave.

"They said I must talk to General Nemesis because they caught me walking around the street with a camera, and I was not a *periodista.*

"I don't know what they thought they would do to me, but I was afraid of this Nemesis because I had seen him once in the Banana Bar in Managua. I thought he must not recognize me.

"I thought they might take money to let me go. But you never know if they will or not.

"I thought, 'Don't fence me in boys, please,' just as they say in the song.

"So they made me sit with them behind some sandbags, actually they were bags full of rice. They had me sitting there with my hands across my head. They took my cigarettes, and let me smoke one, too.

"Another Guard sergeant they call China Dragon he was there, and he had been shot real badly in the foot, and when he removed his boot it was just all full of puss and blood.

"He began to call the people names like 'pimp,' and 'terrorists.' 'Children of whores,' too.

"He was just in a lot of pain, I think, but there was no doctor for him.

"My friend was maybe fifty meters away, all dead, and I thought this China Dragon he was a Nicaraguan, too, just like the sergeant, Macho Negro, but they were no men at all because people like him should be in jail because they take them from the prisons and put them into uniforms to kill our friends, and now they tell us don't kill such people.

"I don't say all, but most. I had no pity for this man. The bone in his foot was shattered. I wished his suffering would not end because I had no pity for him.

"They came and told me then that the General was too busy to see a little jerk like me, and they said I could go back to my house and in the morning come again and ask for a Captain Salazar who would see me, sure, or they would send the China Dragon to get me wherever I was.

"I started away from the Guard *cuartel* and I walked through the little park where there are some swings. I was going maybe to my grandmother's house to rest, and then maybe she would give me supper. Some food to eat.

"So I saw this other pal I once knew and he was not dead at all, and when he saw me and I told him about Rudolfo he said we should go right around the corner and tell the *periodistas* from North America because they would take pictures and make newspaper stories and the government would be made to look terrible to the people of the whole world.

"I was pretty tired, you know, but I said I would, if he came with me.

"I went with him, and just around the corner from the jail near my dead friend was this Yankee journalist, and his friends had movie cameras, too.

"My friend said I should tell them what I had seen.

"I told them about my friend lying dead with a woman and two boys over there and the Yankee he said he had seen them; the Red Cross was coming to cut them open and burn them so the gases could escape.

"Then the man who took photos asked me in Spanish was my friend a Sandinistan?

"'He was crossing the street,' I said.

"'He wasn't fighting?'

"'Maybe so, or maybe he was coming to see me at the fire station.'

"I heard another Yankee say they were only interested in the fighters. They had seen enough civilians. He said, 'We need to find some dead Sandinistan.'

"So because I thought I would do my country a good service I told this Yankee a big lie. I told him my friend was a big Sandinistan, and all the squad leaders wore the yellow sweaters just like him. He was called Number Five...

"'Your friend was a chief?'

"'Sí. Claro, he's dead now, but he was a tiptop rebel for his country, and now he is dead in front of the jail and they have hidden all the soldiers' corpses he made so the people wouldn't see.'

"'Are you a Sandinistan, too?' asked the Yankee.

"'I was hiding all the time in the Fire Station. I am not so crazy that I would kill myself for nothing.'

"'Do you think the Sandinistans kill themselves for nothing?'

"'Nobody knows. Maybe so. Do you?'

"Then I told my other friend we should just go but this Yankee who was really just a German said he would pay me $50 in cordobas right now if I would stand above my dead friend and grieve for him while they took more photos.

"'I don't want to cry. He stinks,' I said. 'And I just don't even want to...'

"Then he said he would give me $60, and all I had to do was look sad.

"I was feeling very angry. But I took the German's money. It's not really important. I just did what he asked me to do. I stood and I pointed and they wanted me to turn the body over, too, so the photos would show Rudolfo's face, but I would not do that.

"I pointed at his yellow sweater that was all dirty with bugs and some blood stains, and the Guard saw us but they didn't stop us from doing that because, you know, all we were doing was pointing at a rotten old dead body."

"*Patria Libre*," added Ramon.

There was simply nothing more he could find to tell me.

"The poverty of this people and their openness, friendliness. They have learned to hate their enemies, not their friends, to discern. I am made welcome to a place my countrymen have helped oppress for a century, but they seem to know the extent to which I am with them, though not of them. Standing in a shack with a hard cold rain coming through the open ceiling, the wife of this poor family offers me their only chair. The husband, an ice-cream vendor, lies in the darkness, coughing sharply, again and again. He has not been able to go out to work in days, at least a week, and no food in the house for the three young children. The woman offers me her chair, to get under the eaves away from the rains.

Today read Sandino was killed by Somoza the year before I was born. I can't be the enemy in that respect, but I am also a Yankee, not a Nicaraguan. M. telling me yesterday: "Rick we need people to worry about us. We will need that all the time."

Nicaraguan diary entry
August, 1978

"Do you bathe in the lake?"
"Yes."
"Is it filthy?"
"Yes."

Nicaraguan diary entry
August, 1978

128

"The hereditary mayor
The chief of police
The commanding general, two hundred troops,
and one school"

From "Ciudad Masaya," by Mario Cajina Vega

"He killed many,
did not take compassion,
all
died
beneath his light,
his terror, his
army"

From "Unnameable One" (Sandino) by Mario Cajina Vega

Pool Politics

Out across the Nicaraguan countryside it was beautiful: misty and soft in the early morning haze, with fertile fields, cattle grazing, high peaks. The lakes took the sunsets aflame, like burning pitch, and the little ruined towns seemed so at peace when washed by the sun or drenched in the rains of almost every afternoon.

Rain is the *guerrilleros*'s best friend: troops don't like to be out in it; and the people stayed indoors under their tin or thatched roofs too; and so—despite the muddy terrain—it was that time when insurgents moved about, beneath a poncho, and raided, and cached themselves somewhere else.

In Nicaragua the insurgents held the cities only so long as it took them to move their forces elsewhere. The people were ransomed for their safety, and they were punished by the soldiers from the air and the ground, and suffered grave hurts, but they didn't go about cursing the rebels. It would be like cursing themselves or the trees. Aliens were among them, the soldiers, and the landscapes of their lives were being uprooted and destroyed by that terror. But the insurgents were like the rains that came in a rush, almost every afternoon, and disappeared again, destructive, and yet replenishing in a way.

They explained for us the cruelty of their fate by saying, "Nicaragua has no friends, and Somoza has more friends in the U.S. Congress than Jimmy Carter."

Or they said, as if listening to themselves speak from a great distance, "Peoples' insurrections with table knives just don't always work so quick," and then continued to hide and give succor to the rebels.

Their lives went on anyway, pretty much as before, conditioned by the usual horrors of normal times: poverty, unemployment, sickness. Once in a small Southern town I followed an ambulance toward the sound of shooting, assuming I would be led to the Sandinistans, but when I found the ambulance parked outside the doorway of a small house I saw only two young attendants resuscitating an old woman.

She sat straight up in a chair in a faded frock, her face and body stiff with terror, her eyes opened so wide they were unblinking: a glass-faced surface of horror.

A resuscitator mask had been placed over her mouth and she seemed to be struggling against it, fighting it and the hands of the attendants, as if they represented the tyranny against which she moaned and gasped and protested and whimpered. I had to glance away at the first sign that her body was relaxing and then I heard the gunfire again, all the way on the other side of the city.

A trench for sewer pipes had been dug in that city and rebels were running about with little pistols shooting at shadows. The guard could not come after them in their armored vehicles; they could not penetrate the guard's defenses. It was a stand-off, scary, because bullets slapped back and forth in between, and I was somewhere in the middle where people were dying from heart attacks as well as *tiroteos*.

Managua was a dead spot in the heart of the countryside that would suddenly fester with heat and noise, explode, and then seem dead once again. It lived in a dead, faded, ruined time: The National Palace, The Ruben Dario Theatre, those art-deco mansion walls crumbling among vacant lots, a bleak gray cathedral, looming so large against the landscape of the polluted lake and bulldozed hills, from which no prayers ever echoed forth any more.

Managua was alive only with expensively-imported Toyotas, and the little cars created traffic jams in which the city stifled and died and the people went about in them with their gossip and their rumors.

The Somozas had all fled to Cocoanut Grove or Acapulco; the Archbishop was in Costa Rica; Commander Zero was dead or in Havana or Peking. The rich, with expensive scanning equipment, monitored the family business of the Somozas over the government radio-telephone frequencies and made recordings; the poor whispered to each other through holes in the walls of the back yards of their barrios, in places they called Las Americas, Bologna, Vietnam.

The rest of the capital was hardly even functional anymore. It had been devastated by an earthquake, and was now paralyzed by a general strike. Its buildings were sprayed with bullet marks. There were patches of rubble on almost every street. The offices of the opposition paper, *La Prensa*, were constantly being armor-plated behind a scaffolding to reduce the risks of strafing attacks from paramilitary assassination squads in passing cars along the *carretera*; even so the offices were destroyed in the last days of the war by point-blank fire from a National Guard tank.

Like Pompeii, or ancient Troy unearthed, or Tikal, or Machu Picchu, parts of Managua seemed in a constant state of excavation. It was a landscape of little bungalows of government employees surviving in rows where handsome villas had been bashed and toppled. The Hotel Intercontinental was a phony modern Mayan pyramid ten stories high; the Somozas' white bombproof bunker next door was slab-like, a tomb with marble bathrooms, and it was dwarfed by a terraced structure, Floridian and flamboyant, where the press received their credentials, and by a concrete monument to the U.S. marines and FDR, surely the Somoza dynasty's two greatest benefactors.

There never was another city as ugly as contemporary

Managua, and it was not going to be rebuilt after the earthquakes, but, instead, added onto, with suburbs for the rich, glossy, and super white, little pastel boxes of concrete for the new middle classes and torn, tacky settlements of squatters' shacks for the poor. The fetid lake often overflowed its shorelines, inundating the homes of barrios Quinta Niña and Acahualinca. There was a constant stench of rot and diesel fumes, garlic, jasmine, and rancid butter.

Even before the curfew was imposed with martial law, many of us felt trapped inside the Hotel Intercontinental. It was hard making friends with Nicaraguans in the middle of a war, and there were very few places to go for amusement. The city gathered in pools of viscous suppuration all about us, and we often dared not wade through it on foot, for fear of the thieves, the pickpockets, the randomly-thrown contact bombs, and the sentries of the National Guard. It was dangerous to be out at night, and certainly scary, as if thirty thousand ghosts were swarming about one's head.

By day, though, there was still all this street life, and people from the city came regularly to the hotel to trade in currency or sex, drugs or souvenirs, to give or get information, to sell news themselves or find out things, or to spy or inform, or just to feel secure nestling among the dubious protections afforded to the foreign press by the "elevated Christian" dictatorship.

There was a certain clubby atmosphere in the bar and the various lounges. The Rotary still met there on alternate Mondays, Dale Carnegie classes met on other days.

On the day Mike Mercenary died with General Allegrette in a plane explosion over Lake Nicaragua, Tom Allen and a UPI photographer and I were all sitting around the outdoor pool, feeling pretty smug and just slightly sad. We'd worked as a team in a couple of the "liberated" cities, and had gotten pretty tight, enough to look out for each other in hairy situations. Were were each others' best chums in Nicaragua.

Mike Mercenary, whose real name was Echannes, had always warned people he thought he was going to buy it, someday, from official sources, and he had been a sort of friend to the press, pretty helpful to some with news and gossip about the Somozas and the generals. We really weren't that sorry to see him go, just saddened by the bad news. It meant anybody could die in Nicaragua, and made all of us feel our own mortality just a little.

Having just returned from a firefight in Diriamba, only half an hour away from Managua, none of us had felt like doing any more work on that sunny warm day, and we settled on lunch by the pool, and maybe a swim after.

There weren't many other people around; the press were all out somewhere witnessing the latest massacre; they would come back to talk of all the horrors they'd seen in the only truly first-class air-conditioned bar in the capital while waiters in blood-red bus jackets passed platters of hot hors d'oeuvres among them.

That afternoon at the shallow end of the pool a mother was teaching her two young boys how to hold on to the sides of the pool and kick. She was dark from the sun and a little overweight. She was wearing a ridiculous, white-sequined bathing cap and she kept telling the boys that when their father got back from his business in the city they must show him their progress.

The only other person in the pool area, aside from the Indian boy who gave us our towels, was a faded, rather skimpy-looking British journalist with large knobby sunburned knees.

He sat under a beach umbrella, wore a sun visor and bermuda shorts, and kept copying things from the *Wall Street Journal* onto a yellow pad using a big orange Waterman pen.

None of us knew this guy's name or for whom he worked, as he wasn't one of the regular bar flies, and some people said he might be a spook, since he never spoke to any of us and never came to look at any of the battles with us. It was rumored that he concentrated on financial news for a London syndicate, but once in the elevator when I asked what he thought was being done with all the wealth in the country, he mumbled, "Sorry, old boy," and turned and glanced the other way.

That happened a lot in Managua; nobody really seemed to know who anybody else was. But that day, Tom Allen and I were talking about the sad decline of the Boston Red Sox when Davey Hartwich from Sigma stepped out onto the patio, saw us, waved, and came over to our table, and then said he would like to buy the next round of drinks in memory of Mike Mercenary who had just crashed and died, according to Government Communiqué #37.

We thought, at first, he was putting us on with a rumor, but he passed the communiqué around and said he was pretty certain it had not been an accident because the general, Allegrette, was in the plane, too, and he had just spoken to a friend in the Guard and this fellow told him the bodies were all in bits and pieces, as after a big explosion.

Davey said, "Mike was really all right, you know. He just happened to be working for the wrong side and I guess he even knew it after a while but the Sandinistans couldn't afford him. He was getting 1200 a week from the Somozas..."

"He told Evelyn two grand," said Tom.

"What difference does it make," went Dave. "It was a heck of a lot of money."

"Well he was a professional at what he did, I suppose," I said.

"Poor schmuck," said Dave.

He was talking about Mike, but I happened to be looking at this new person who had stepped out onto the patio from the bar. He started to strip off his street clothes until his dark lean body was covered only with a small blue French *cache sex*, or bikini, and when he turned around toward the pool all of us, including the woman in the pool, saw a rather large scab, like a jumpsuit zipper, extending from his pelvis up practically to his right shoulder.

It looked as if somebody had slashed this wound across his chest with a bayonet and it was just very ugly and also a little off-putting.

"Get a load of that poor son-of-a-bitch," I observed. The others grunted, but as this guy stepped gingerly down into the wading end of the pool I heard the woman chatter shrilly, and then I saw her gather the two children and herd them quickly out of the water.

Davey said, "Looks like bad trouble."

Sure enough, the woman stepped out of the pool herself and turned on this young guy and rattled off a harsh noisy volley of invectives.

It was too fast for me to get all of it, so Davey started to translate, more or less paraphrasing as he went along.

"She says he is unclean and must not bring his filthy body with its wounds into this pool. Her children will catch an infection. She calls him viperous, a poison... as one Nicaraguan to another, mind you."

The fellow was standing thigh deep in the shallows with his hands on his hips and he just took it, without saying anything back. Neither did he make any effort to leave the pool.

"Filth, she calls him," Davey explained, "and pustu ...lation I guess."

Tom said, "I wonder if it's a class or a caste thing?"

"It's a war thing," I said. "That guy looks like he was wounded fighting."

Finally the woman seemed to grow discouraged. She pushed the two small boys who were behind her toward their cabana to dress, abandoning the large clear blue pool to the man with his zipper scab, who frowned and dunked himself once more in a squat and rose up again and dunked down a second time.

Davey said, "I'm gonna find out what that was all about."

He went around to the other side of the pool and crouched down and addressed himself to the bather.

Presently the guy waded his way across to one of the ladders and climbed up out of the pool and Davey handed him his towel and he draped it across his shoulders and started walking with Davey over toward our table.

"Fellows," Davey said, "this is Lieutenant Salvatore of the Nicaraguan National Guard. He's kindly accepted our invitation to have a drink. The lieutenant was wounded when the Sandinistas took Penas Blancas briefly . . . "

"Really?"

"No shit," said Tom.

Salvatore nodded darkly, gravely, handsomely and sat down among us.

I said, "You're lucky to be alive lieutenant."

"I should say I am," he replied, blinking his eyes.

When the barman came to take our orders the lieutenant ordered a double Scotch with soda, which is very expensive in Nicaragua, and since we were paying I decided to get our money's worth from him, as soon as possible.

"So? How's El Mayor?"

"He is ok, Tachito," the lieutenant grinned: "Don't you believe all those rumors."

Tom said, "We heard Tachito was in Europe talking to the new Pope."

"He's here. Who ever said Rome?" The lieutenant seemed just a little quarrelsome.

Dave asked: "And the old man? The Boss?"

"Everything is normal I tell you," said the lieutenant. He grinned as his tall frosty drink was set before him, and that scab seemed to darken on his very first prim sip.

I said, "As normal as that tatoo you got across your chest."

"That was a different story," he said. "The raid . . . that was something truly different . . . but I am here to tell you about it . . . we will survive."

He seemed so very cocky I couldn't help but add, "With some help from Uncle Sam."

"And Israel," Tom put in.

"Brazil, too." The lieutenant would not be goaded. "Nicaragua has friends," he said. "The terrorists have only Cuba."

I asked, "Which terrorists would you be talking about?"

He grinned at me slyly. "You keeding me?"

"Sure," went Dave, "we were just keeding. But you know about Allegrette and Mike Mercenary..."

"Yes." He suddenly looked very weary and sad, and just a little desperate for our good opinion of him. "It is very bad what happened as they were good soldiers and it is not a good thing at all."

"Do you think it was an accident?"

"What do you think?" asked Salvatore. He leaned forward on his elbows just as Dave loudly barked at him, "Hah."

Then we were all silent in the sun. I thought to myself the lieutenant was very handsome, like a young god, except for his new wound, which crossed his body like a cartridge belt, and gave him, even naked and wet, the very martial and imperious air of a young Roman.

A woman from Agence France-Press came out onto the patio and was coaxed into joining us. She said there was "fighting going on right now at kilometer 5 on the southern highway," but nobody wanted to go with her to see what was happening.

The lieutenant said the "terrorists are desperate." We knew he had to say such things to us.

Then I asked why the woman in the pool had hassled him so.

"What do you mean?" he asked.

"That woman with her kids," I said. "She seemed really pissed at you, if you know what I mean."

The lieutenant frowned: "They don't know what they want this people they never know."

I said nothing.

He said, "She is the daughter of Armando Pellear. To her we are none of us good enough."

"Is that all?" went Tom.

I asked who Armando Pellear was and was told the family was one of Nicaragua's leading landowners and very close to the Boss.

Dave said, "So you got wounded defending her ass, and now she doesn't want you in the pool with your scab."

"*Ya lo creo,*" said the lieutenant, smirking. "She is just a silly woman. Sometimes I think such people deserve the Sandinistans... but I am not as you say political. I am anti-political, how you say, and it is not my business. I have nothing but contempt for such people. I fight for myself and my mother. She would not like to live under the Communists."

"Are you sure?" asked Tom.

"It is only my opinion," said the lieutenant. "Personally I have nothing against Commander Zero. He is a very brave soldier. But my mother gets older. She deserves her comforts, and there would be no place for me in such a Nicaragua. They have said so."

I wanted to add: only if you have committed "crimes" against the people. But I restrained myself. He might have, because most had done so, at one time or another, doing their duty for the Boss and his son. For such a brave and easy-going fellow the lieutenant seemed fearful.

We were really at the point where we had used the lieutenant to his limits. He wasn't about to divulge any governmental secrets, even if he knew any, and I wanted a nap and a shower. Then maybe I could do some writing.

I called out for the check, and my two colleagues reached into their pockets for money.

"...I would like a tempest of blood, for the hour of the rehabilitation of social justice to be sounded... The spirit of the lower classes shall embody an implacable future vengeance. One shall have to sing a new Marseillaise which, like the trumpets of Jericho, destroyed those infamous walls. Fires will ignite the old ruins and there one shall see the rich begging clemency of the poor... the supreme and terrible vengeance of a drunken misery...

"But who are you? Why do you say such things? I call myself Juan Lanas, and I don't have a dime."

**Letter from Nicaraguan poet Ruben Dario
Published in the *Herald of Costa Rica*
March 17, 1892**

Getting out of the elevator on my floor of the hotel, I see two soldiers armed with automatic rifles leaving my room.

They slam and fasten the door shut and see me.

I don't ask where they've been or what they were doing. Assume they had the pass key.

We pass in the hall as if we had nothing to do with each other.

In the room everything seems to be just as I had left it. But there is a feeling of fear, worse than before: bewildered by this apparent violation, I wander about the room, checking to see that everything is still in place: a book, a dirty shirt, a little cassette recorder.

Nothing has been altered, it seems. So why did they come to my room? And what were they doing?

Evacuation of a city: whole families, parrots, guerrille-ros. *Those who are stopped are vouched for by others and pass quickly through the roadblock of soldiers.*

They seem bewildered and, when you talk to them, they express open anger.

The press reports only their bewilderment.

Hard for these sophisticated cosmopolitan journalists to understand that people without credit cards and literacy can still have a coherent political position.

Very simply, they hate the regime for what it has done to them day by day and year by year.

They have been humiliated and ripped off, and now they are being made homeless by planes and soldiers.

As one man said to me, "Even before the Yankees came, and the Somozas, we all lived here, and we were a people ...we were Nicaraguans...and these were our homes."

September 16, 1978

"Wasn't Nicaragua wonderful once upon a time?" When she was just a little girl, the poet Ruben Dario wrote love poems to the first Somoza's future wife. My friend Luis is related to that woman, too, whom people call Yo Ya; and babies died and were buried in an open field next door to the monuments in the National Cemetery. Ruben Dario wrote the first Mrs. Somoza when she was just a little girl: Be careful how you lose you heart. He couldn't have been more right. Everybody is a cousin of everybody else, it seems, down here, which never stopped murder, I think, and may only go to prove why the Communists are right when they say blood isn't thicker than water: that beautiful young Sandinistan over there is the daughter of a National Guard general. And the couple who were stopped in the shack outside León because the man had a

hunting rifle in the back of his car were distant cousins of Tacho, as it turned out, which is why they got away with their contraband when Major Salazar had searched their car, and I am almost certain they intended to bring that weapon to a guerrillero, *if they were not* guerrilleros *themselves. "Adam" telling me "in the mountains we eat lizards, when we catch them." "Very sweet flesh." ...And Major Salazar (who later became Commander Bravo) telling me the war would stop if only Panama stopped sending weapons such as the French self-propelled rocket he showed me.*

**...From My Notebooks
September, 1978**

General Allegrette's Burial

The burial of General Allegrette was held in the National Cemetery in Managua, not very far away from the Somoza family tombs, which were once shadowed by a giant monument of a Nicaraguan National Guardsman, with his legs spread slightly apart, in combat dress, a fecal shade of brown.

Most of the important people in Managua, at the time, came to the interment, including the Chilean Ambassador and the Ambassador from Taiwan and the last Somoza's son, "El Mayor", Tachito, who was, at 27, a commander-in-chief of the National Guard, Captain Earthquake, as people called him. A lot of important people were saying the Somozas had blown up General Allegrette's plane over Lake Nicaragua because the General was capable and popular, but too ambitious for the Somozas; so an appearance by somebody from the Family was a matter of *comme il faut*; and, as it was a bit too risky for the old man to appear in any public place, in plain air, he sent his son, along with some of his young officers trained in the Canal Zone, to watch the other generals who were pallbearers put what was left of General Jose Ivan Allegrette into the ground.

Next to Tachito, who is big and boyish with a bland face, one of these young officers always stood; he was a frail wiry little fellow with coppery skin and large jug ears. He was a captain and he came up to Tachito's armpits. With those big fan-like elephant ears, he looked as if you could lift his whole body stiffly up toward your shoulders by just grabbing a hold by those two *orejas*. When they stood at attention together for the slow shuffle and drag of the cadets in immaculate whites and the fly-by of the Spanish turbo-props of the Nicaraguan *Fuerza Aerea*, Ears kept glancing up at the boss' son, as if to find out how to comport himself.

The day was clear, warm, a perfect afternoon in "little summer," and they both wore spotless military pinks, dead ringers for American GI summer chinos except for those small Nicaraguan silver wedges they used as insignia to replace our USAs. The creases of their garments couldn't have been sharper, Gung-ho, such as Jody in the old Fort Dix songs never was: spit-polished black brogues, and neat new shade-44 green ties with Windsor knots.

Well, a lot of dirt was being dropped into the grave by the widow and her daughters, blondes all of them, and by a boy with teased hair who looked as if he had just been catapulted from St. Tropez for the ceremonies. He had vague blurry eyes, as if he was staring through drops. Many of the relatives wore mink capes or stoles, and the men who were not in the military wore shiny black-and-gray silk moleskin suits.

Tachito and his aide were about ten feet away from the mourners. Even when they were not standing at attention they looked a little too stiff, as if their faces had been encased in acrylic fixative. There was some discreet wailing and moaning. A military chaplain commended the soul of General Allegrette to Jesus Christ. The Generals huffed and puffed and slid a handsome wooden box six feet into a hole in the ground.

Then things started to break up, with groups of people going different ways, but a big crowd was gathered around the hole to watch some workmen seal it with cement.

There were two scruffy Indian fellows who dropped

down into the hole on ropes and started trouncing about on top of the box. They slid a concrete lid across the narrow crypt, and then, like chefs preparing a pâté, spread it all over with dark wet cement. One of their trowels went a little wild when people started to disperse, and this tiny gobbet of stuff sailed up out of the open grave, and through a gap in the crowd, landing with big wet sop just above Ear's right cuff.

Looked just like a little piece of sick wet baby shit, and must have felt kind of sticky, too, just like sick wet baby shit.

I think he thought it was shit, too, so dark against his pinks, because at first he didn't seem to want to give it any official notice, much less touch it; and then Tachito saw it and his nose wrinkled, the closest thing to an emotion I'd seen registered there throughout the ceremony; and then his lips moved once, a little, and Ears heard and obeyed, immediately scraped some of it off with a fingernail and brought it up to his nose.

You could tell he still wasn't sure what the stuff was then because his nose was wrinkling, too, when he started to flip it away to one side of him, and then he saw there would be this wet spot; and he began to scrape away at it, and rub, and scrape, first with his fingers, then with a large white hanky.

Pretty soon there was just this dark spot which really showed because it had spread so much from all that rubbing.

By now, Tachito had walked off elsewhere; he was too disgusted to stick around any more next to such a fuck-up. He was shaking hands with some other officers and their ladies and bowing a little, stiffly, right in the middle of this warm September afternoon; and when Ears straightened up and joined him at last, Tachito only moved on a bit again, toward another crowd of people, as if to tell the fellow, "You've been shat on, not me, Pal, so kindly do something about it, and don't hang around me any more until you have."

That poor little captain really looked like he was in disgrace, and all because of a spot on his trousers. He kept staring at the ground and trying to get closer to Tachito who kept moving away to another group of people. Finally he went over, all alone, to a woman in basic black with pearls to get himself a hug, and she also backed off.

It must have gotten around he had shit on his pants. There'd be no *abrazos* for Ears.

Everybody started out through the wrought-iron gates of the National Cemetery in different small cabals of mourner-gossipers toward their Mercedeses; but just as I was leaving with them a small, bare procession of mourners entered, lugging a tiny gray cardboard coffin.

They had come on foot from the city in two single files, about sixteen people, the women in shabby black dresses or sweaters, with bunches of wild flowers, the men who carried the coffin also shouldering pickaxes and shovels.

The child was two years old, one man told me. She had died of a fever because she did not receive the proper medical attention in time.

Crying out, choking...

Death is something we all must share, eventually. But none of the official mourners for General Allegrette even seemed to take notice of this new burial party of the poor. A stout woman with a frayed shawl across her shoulders was weeping and the sound she suddenly made, though soft enough, seemed to carry against the noise of expensive motors revving.

A brawny, bare-foot fellow, red-faced and drunk, wore brief shabby work pants that only came up to his calves, and he looked like a character in a Lope de Vega comedy, but, though he panhandled me for some *reales* as soon as he caught my eye, he did not ask for backsheesh from any of the prosperous-looking official guests.

The rest of that dingy mourning party moved on without him, and did not wait for him to catch up. With their small cardboard casket, they seemed very anxious to get away from all the Guardsmen providing security during the General's burial.

I followed after this party of the poor. They went down the main aisle of graves and monuments, passing General Allegrette's new crypt banked high with flowers, and almost under the legs of that towering brown Guardsman erected above the Somozas, until they had come to a much more modest section of the cemetery where there were very few stone monuments, not even stone or wooden crosses.

They went off into a wasteland beyond, overgrown with grass and weeds, and while some men commenced to break the soil and dig, others—including some women— held the little box aloft.

I started to join them there, but they gave me a hard no-trespassing stare that made me hold my ground and turn away again toward the main gate.

A small man in a blue business suit and blue tie was standing in the middle of the path, under the shadow cast by the Somoza monument. He crooked his finger at me once, then twice again.

He looked to be in his early sixties and he spoke careful English. "You are *periodista* journalist?" He didn't seem frightening, but almost reassuring. Such a paltry pasty figure in dapper blue: "*¿Periodista?*" he repeated.

"Yes."

"But you don't wear your badge."

"I know."

"Do you even have a badge?"

"Yes."

"Well then give it to me and I will pin it on for you."

I obeyed this little gray-haired man as if I were a child and he were my father, and though I had to bend over and flex my knees, because he could not reach up to my chest otherwise, I did not feel at all reprimanded, but somehow startled and pleased that someone was taking care of me. The pin of the plastic press badge pricked the skin of my chest at first, and when I winced I smelled the faintest odor of Yardley talc, with which my own father used to dust his face after a shave. And then I noticed this man also wore a small gold pin in the lapel of his suit; it was a Rotary International pin.

Seeing my eyes take in the pin, the little man smiled dimly up at me and said, "I work in a bank. You might say I am a banker."

There was a slight throbbing in his thin voice, but his eyes were dry; his bare cheeks flaky, and the exaggerated care with which he spoke to me in English seemed to suggest that he was taking great pains that I get his meaning.

"It could be dangerous for you to be here without your badge," he told me. "People they don't always understand if you come to places like this who you are."

"Agreed." I felt slightly addled by so much talk.

He stood back and surveyed the work of his hands on my chest with some pride.

"See? You are a journalist. So you have a badge, and you wear it. Bueno señor..."

The little man's smile faded on him. He looked like a creature of talc.

"Well so now I must go to find my son...and say hello!"

"He's waiting for you?"

"He always waits. He is buried...back there somewhere."

He pointed off toward an area of modest monuments that ended abruptly just before the wilderness of the potter's field commenced.

"He died some years back," he added, absently, "and whenever I am here I always try to go and see him for a minute or two."

I nodded. With our eyes we dismissed each other.

"Good day, sir."

"*Buenas,*" I said back.

"*Suerte,*" he replied, "and always please remember to wear your badge from now on."

He disappeared behind a monument on which some street kids were playing King of the Mountain, and just then another small procession in black carrying another gray cardboard child's coffin was starting down the main aisle of the cemetery toward me.

Managua's Only French Restaurant

There used to be one pretty good French restaurant in Managua, Nicaragua, called La Gauloise, just like the cigarette, in a residential part of town, on a quiet street, opposite the home of the Inspector General for Aqueducts, Debayle Martinez.

It wasn't a very large place, the front parlor of a private home, and it was very expensive for Nicaragua: nothing, not even the soups, cost less than thirty cordobas (four dollars).

The owner, Alain Marie, was a former merchant seaman from Brittany who'd "married" one of the local women and gone into the food business. He was quite successful for a while. A lot of top government people and generals turned up there for dinner with their wives and girlfriends; his regular customers also included Robelo, leader of the middle-class Broad Opposition Front to the Somoza government, other prominent businessmen, most of the foreign press corps, and a certain well-known writer of *belles lettres* who was said to be, in some way, close to the Sandinistan rebels.

La Gauloise was declared neutral territory after the shooting started up. You could eat there feeling almost as if you were on French soil. Enemies sat in different parts of the room, aware of each other, even as they nodded over their plates of snails with garlic. Nobody was ever hassled by anybody while eating at La Gauloise, but there were often squads of elite Black Beret soldiers and pro-government paramilitary thugs posted on the dark streets nearby to intercept certain diners leaving the place. For that reason, Alain Marie, the patron, would often allow clandestines and politicos to exit by his kitchen door in the back of the house.

"I am a *restauranteur*, not a politician," Alain Marie would explain, "and I need to keep every customer I have. I don't want to lose you. I don't want to lose any of you. Believe me."

But everybody suspected he was a rebel sympathizer. People even said his wife's sister was a girlfriend of the rebel Tomas Borge.

That was never proved to my satisfaction. I believe Alain Marie was, in the true sense of the term, an "accommodating person," and he was hoping to accommodate his facilities and menu to whichever regime took power.

French people are sometimes like that, I suppose. I divide them into roughly two distinct classes: those who are hearty and accommodating, and those who are mean. Alain Marie was not a very good cook; he covered everything he made with garlic and tomatoes and then labeled it "*à la provençal*," or he daubed it over with a white cream sauce and insisted it was a *béarnaise*; but he always tried to be open, friendly, hospitable, generous with his portions. It wasn't his fault the ruling Somoza dynasty had such heavy import duties on wines and spirits that an ordinary bottle of claret cost the customer twenty dollars. He made the least of his profits from wines. He served French wines because his customers insisted on it, and most could afford to pay the going price.

Everybody had been lining their pockets in Managua for years with what was and what was not available, and for how much. So, whenever you complained about his prices, Alain Marie, like a true citizen of his adopted country, would shrug his shoulders and blame it all on the Somoza family, particularly Tacho, the dictator.

Fair enough!

The new ten percent tax on restaurant service wasn't going into Alain Marie's pockets.

Nor did he get a share of the heavy new taxes on his canned snail shells.

Somebody had to pay for this war. The Somozas wouldn't, so the Nicas did, rich and poor, on both sides of the political battle.

And Alain Marie had plenty of his own headaches. He, too, was being exploited: by the army captains and lieutenants and majors who ate meals in his place wearing combat dress and sidearms and demanding complimentary service.

When the curfew came into effect, he had very few customers left, and he started closing at seven-thirty in the evening so that people could be home before eight, the hour when his place was normally jumping.

Then his wife miscarried, and his son's school was closed for weeks because of the general strike, and his daughter was not accepted into the rhythmical gymnastics team, and it was harder and harder to get decent fresh provisions, and his farm, near Jinotepe, lost its coffee crop when the frightened migrant workers refused to come up north from Rivas. He was going broke; his big white Citroen, identical to Tachito's, the Boss' son's, was more or less permanently disabled for lack of spare parts. He had labor troubles, a bleeding hemorrhoid, an errant girlfriend, and that was just the start of all his griefs...

Alain Marie wore a worried face like some people crown their heads with blow-dried hair styles. His business fears gave him an increasingly dry look, a pasty face.

You'd be eating supper, and he would come over to your table to give you his host's greeting, and what you also got then, compulsively, inadvertently, were complaints, harangues, shoulder shrugs, and proprietary curses.

It wasn't good for the digestion or proper enjoyment of his mediocre cuisine, so then Alain Marie would always add: "Ah well, monsieur, it is these *bims* (bombs), and the bastards who run this place. You know. It's terrible..."

"Of course..."

"*Bien sûr,*" he would add. "That coward Somoza..."
But two tables away a high minister of the government
might be seated and a couple of hookers, so that it almost
seemed to be Alain Marie's intention to be overheard, with
the press as his only witness and shield.

One night, during the battle for León, I was having a
late supper at La Gauloise with a photographer from
Time, and Alain Marie came specially over to our table to
offer us each a glass of *eau-de-vie* on the house.

I asked how things were with him.

"*Perfecto!*"

"You seemed very worried two nights ago," the woman
from *Time* reminded him.

"Why should I not?" he demanded, resuming his custom-
arily haggard air. "This war will destroy everything. Look
at my restaurant. Aside from you there is only a man from
the police having dinner here tonight."

We looked over to a table at the far end of the room
where a tiny pale man with a pencil mustache bent over
his heaping plate of stew as if he had cramps.

"Alain," I asked, "what's so perfect about that?"

He replied, "My friend, for me this is a perfect disaster,
no?"

He told us then, in a whisper, that the fellow had
appeared every night in the week for his supper at this
hour "and because of him I must stay open."

"*What about us?*" asked my woman friend.

"You don't do this," said Alain Marie, making a slitting
gesture with his finger across his throat.

The cop was masticating on a large chunk of pork.

Again Alain Marie whispered, "Coward."

"Cool it," we said. As if he didn't know that. He really
didn't seem to wish to be discreet any longer.

When we came back to La Gauloise a few nights later
the restaurant was closed for business. A hand-lettered
sign on the massive wooden front door read: "Due to the

current emergency, La Gauloise can no longer provide service."

We were disappointed. Even though the food wasn't that good, it was a place to go to to get away from the hotel and the gossip and all the government spies in the lobby. I felt so much more a prisoner in Nicaragua for having been denied the possibility of further meals at La Gauloise, but I went on with my work and my life and really thought no more of Alain Marie and his problems until the day after the government had retaken the city of Estelí in the north. The following morning I went to the airport to find a "pigeon" who could smuggle out some copy for me. The Somozas had just pulled the plug on the communications satellite, disconnected the telex, and imposed complete press pre-censorship. No news was supposed to leave Managua without government approval. I didn't trust the phones, so I had to use pigeons.

A blonde Mormon girl from the Peace Corps was flying to Miami, and she agreed to take my sealed envelope and give it to a man on the other side of the customs desk. I felt pretty smart about what I had done and was just about to boogie my way back to the hotel when I saw Alain Marie.

He stood in a pale flaccid sweat on the Pan Am standby line, which was no line at all, but a crush, a mob scene.

He was all by himself. He had just two smart Saint-Laurent suitcases, and a pale suit jacket with the lining turned out across his forearm.

He was leaving Nicaragua, without his family. I didn't ask why. He waved his fingers discreetly in my direction.

"So nice of you to come," he said, reaching out to hug me to his sweaty shirtfront.

I complied, but just barely, and then he added: "I understand, It is *not* pleasant waiting here."

I inquired if he planned to be away a long time.

"Forever," he crooned. "Always and forever..."

"And your...people?" I asked, not wishing to get too personal.

Alain Marie said, "Ask President Somoza."

Again he shrugged.

He didn't seem that uncomfortable about running out; he was a Frenchman and Nicaraguans had a more difficult time bribing officials for their passports.

Probably he could do more for his family from outside the border, I thought.

So I asked what he planned to do with all his property, the restaurant, the house and car, the cases of wine and spirits.

Again Alain Marie gave me that drenching fat glazed look, a look of sadness and passivity, and said, more fiercely, "Ask Tacho Somoza..."

"You will go back to France?"

"It is unlikely," he observed. "There I am not such a good chef..."

"Where then?"

"Perhaps I shall become a rebel..."

"Don't make jokes, Alain," I said, as loudly as possible.

He glanced about to make sure he was not being overheard and said, "In El Salvador I could be a good French chef...

"You know," he winked, "in El Salvador a good French chef from Nicaragua is considered a genius..."

"Of that I am certain," I told him. "But there's terror there, too, and the "White Hand." In the end the same things may happen there..."

"*Claro*," went Alain Marie. He nodded briskly at me with his chin as a big bead of sweat dripped down off of it.

"In the meantime," he said then, "we live this way, people like us..."

"The fortunes of war," I said.

"*Oui Perfecto*," went Alain Marie.

I said goodbye, and wished him luck. I knew he would need it. To be an itinerant in the middle of a revolution is bad enough, being less than a genius at what you do makes it even worse.

I hoped no dissatisfied customer in El Salvador blew him away after a meal, but I felt he would probably get by, in the meantime, as he had been doing all his life: by accommodating.

My little pigeon never showed up in Miami with my copy.

She thought I was a communist spy or a dangerous terrorist, so she turned it over to an airline captain who gave it to the Somozan government.

An Incident in León

At one point in the struggle against Somoza, his own National Guard was able, in the language of a communiqué, to "recuperate" the ancient city of León. The rebels all went underground or fled, and the people of the city were left without any food or water. When they came into the streets from their battered houses to share their terrors, they told stories to anybody who would listen; stories of indiscriminate bombings and strafings, of certain young men and boys being rounded up and, with their hands fastened behind their backs, machine-gunned to death by elite killer squads of Guardsmen and paramilitaries.

All the barricades built up before were being demolished by big orange government bulldozers, and some of us in the press were promised safe conduct by the Guard if we agreed not to stray too far from the main avenues of the city.

My friends and I returned to the old city with the hope of finding certain of our friends in León, people we had met and thought we knew a little and cared about. Food was still scarce everywhere, so we brought only what we could buy from the hotel to give as presents to these people to eat: huge whipped-cream cakes and Sacher tortes, fruit pies, expensive chicken box lunches. Laden down, wav-

ing white flags, we made our way past all the final road
blocks and walked in single file along the cobbled streets,
intrepid Lady Bountifuls, hoping to locate these old
friends.

There was a great deal of street life milling about. Each
greeting was an acknowledgment that one had survived
with hope and defiance intact. But occasional sniper fire
kept going off in the adjacent barrios, like billiard balls
caroming.

Around the market place, we had also been told, the
Guard was shooting into the air to scare off hungry people
who might be looting.

The people on the streets, after we had relieved ourselves of our packages, showed us all the numerous
freshly-dug graves in their back yards, and the holes they
had dug into back-yard adobe walls so that they could
communicate during the bombardments with some de-
gree of safety.

I met very few Somocistas on the streets of León that
day, or any other day.

A woman on the street told me, "If we ever are victorious
I shall learn how to read because they will teach us. Then
we will be able to read all the things you write about us
here today, meester."

Wherever I walked, the sound of my sandals slapping
against cobblestones punctuated aimless spatters of distant random gunfire. I felt as if I had walked barefoot
across a lake of ice. The soles of my feet and the back of my
neck felt numb and burnt. Bright noonday heat made me
ache all over. I was slick with my own sweat, queasy.

How would it feel, I wondered as I walked, to be picked
off by a stray round or ricochet? Would I know I was dead
before the vertigo, the blood?

"Death most quickly singles out he who is afraid of
death," Sandino reportedly once said. But so deep was my
apprehensiveness that I wandered away from my American friends, as if asking be singled out, and found myself
alone, after a while, in the market place.

A number of young girls and older women, in black shawls, rummaged the ashy debris of a storefront that had once traded in *aguadiente* and Ron Flor De Cana.

Some had collected as many as twenty or even thirty fire-blackened pint bottles in little piles along the cobblestones. Others stood very still, jiggling them inside large black shawls, like eggs or contact bombs. A few older women were stooping low over the ash heaps. They waded in deeply so that their black shoes and the hems of their skirts had a coating of ash.

A teenaged girl stood to one side, guarding a small pile of the bottles she and her friends or mother had liberated.

When I walked near by she said she would gladly sell me a bottle for twenty cordobas (about two dollars).

Like a creature in a Goya painting, her pose was seductive, with a large black mantilla draped across her forehead. She had very soft and full rosy cheeks, as if she'd rouged them, and the most luxurious thick eyelashes shadowing big brown eyes. Aside from the heavy black cowl in which she had enveloped her head, she was dressed like any other teenager of our era: in jeans, a polo shirt, and sneakers.

"Listen," she told me, as if hipping me to be as street wise as she, "this is the authentic stuff that only lacks a label because of fire. Be brave m*ee*ster."

"No thank you."

"Why not?"

"I am a bit of a weakling when it comes to *aguadiente*."

"You are not the only one," she told me, smirking.

She started to giggle, just like a teenager, and that made my neck unfreeze, momentarily.

She batted her eyelashes.

I realized we were flirting, as on any other street, in any other place in the world.

"Oh," she told me then, "you don't look like such a weakling to me. Maybe you're just a choosy person. Are you North American?"

"Yes."

"It's important that you came to León today," she told me, "Because the whole world must bear witness to all this."

It was said with a toss of her head, a little drama, and then she spread out her arms, too, so that the scarf fell backward off her forehead, and then again she laughed, as if she had experienced such good feeling for me, and it made her feel good, too.

Her gaze, resting on my face, made my cheeks burn a little. I could feel her glance laving me, a fresh breeze along that stifling midday street.

"If I don't buy," I asked her, "what will you do with all these bottles?"

"That's for my mother to decide."

She motioned with her chin at the bent back of a heavy woman in dark clothing who leaned far into one of the ash heaps, sorting noisily.

The woman heard us talking about her. She didn't stand up or even turn around, but showed us her face, dark with blood, from bending over.

"*Venga,*" she seemed to bark, upside down, at her daughter, who immediately left me to go toward her.

I could overhear them debating whether or not it was wise to be talking to strangers, and it was just as strange to me, in the midst of so much devastation, to be reminded of such old-fashioned attitudes of some Nicaraguan mothers with their daughters, of eyes batting and commands, reproaches, in the middle of such a former battleground.

"He's just much too old for you, this man," the woman said then, and, suddenly, as if to reproach all of us, came the noise of automatic weapons, fired quite close by.

"Love of God," shouted another woman, hoarsely, and she ran from the ash heaps for cover, along with all the others, leaving me standing quite alone next to a pile of bottles.

A woman had dropped a small black-and-silver paper fan, with a gilded plastic handle. It lay to my left in the gutter, half spread out, less than ten feet from where I stood, its outermost blades barely touching a sticky stain of grease or blood which was being buzzed over by large gold-and-black-and-bluish flies.

Even though I wanted to retrieve the fan, I was afraid to move. Stood there sticking to all the empty glare of that street.

My friends had told me never to run when the shooting started. The soldiers would think I was one of the rebels and shoot me down. So when the next volley of shots resounded quite close by, I fell down hard against the pavement.

Hot cobblestones pressed against my belly and chest and cheeks. Shots came louder, closer. Some people in doorways on both sides of the street were shouting at me in Spanish to find cover, and motioning with their hands. I saw the girl and her mother huddling together in a door-way underneath a shattered Telefunken sign, and I remained in my exposed place on the street next to this large pile of contraband bottles and a small broken fan, and all I could think was: Don't Run. Please don't run, Richard.

The Guard jeep appeared at the intersection, and another volley of shots slapped against the buildings over-head. They were not using rubber bullets. A dust of acrid plaster drifted downward. A soldier fired off his whole clip sounding like a cross-cut saw against heavy metal.

There were three soldiers sitting in the jeep, and another was standing behind a .50-caliber machine gun that pointed out the rear of the vehicle.

They had propped their weapons skyward, and were just squeezing off round after round and then reloading to fire again, as if to keep all the people they passed on the streets scared.

As they turned our corner and headed down the long flat block on which I was stretched out, I saw the clear flash of a large clear glass bottle being raised heavenward in the front seat of the car. Brakes screeched, and the jeep lurched tipsily forward.

Their tires made a sucking sound as they came even closer. I had sprung a slow leak, was wheezing breath. I believed they would surely run right over me, if they did not shoot me first.

But I had been cautioned, again and again, not to run.

That jeep came bearing down hard at me and, as if to ward off its impact, I began to yell: *"Periodista. Norte Americano periodista. Ayuda me..."*

But then I got up on my knees and began to move, rising higher into a crouch and running as fast as I could for the girl and her mother and the cover of their doorway.

No room where they stood, so they pushed me sideways as more shots went off, and the people in the next doorway all seemed to reach out to me, at once stepping away from their cover to pull me toward them, until I was by their side, could smell them all and even feel their heat and the touch of their hands and bodies, the gussets of their warm breath whenever they spoke to me.

"Don't be afraid. Rest here and don't move."

A big bomb went off somewhere nearby, rattling windows and shaking the walls of the building in which we all huddled. But none of us cowered.

A stout Indian fellow next to me wagged his finger at my face. "You must learn to move with the others when they move. It's a matter of reflexes... to watch the others and do as they do."

More shots went off, as the patrol proceeded down the block, and I asked, "Are they really just firing at the sky?"

"They wish us to remain frightened of them," a woman explained, "You'll see. There are not enough of them to patrol every street always."

"You'll see," the man said, "it's happening already... *Mira...*"

And at that moment people began to step away from their doorways and were milling about in the streets once more. They were smiling, laughing. Nobody had been hurt. Some scavengers returned to their labor of sorting through the ash heaps, and others began to pile up heavy paving blocks and pieces of wrecked building to construct another new barricade.

When the last of my companions left me to go about his business, I felt a little bereft, abandoned, as if, having glimpsed the grace of our common existence, I could not be excluded any longer.

I wanted to follow some to their clandestine meeting places, lift cobblestones for more new barricades.

On the sunny street my own shadow surprised me, warring with the shadow of a ragged young boy who was standing under my elbow and pulling at my hand.

Smiling, he inquired would the *periodista* care to see a corpse in a grocery store window.

It had happened last night near the Hospital San Vicente.

Mira venga.

III

October 1979

*"I'm too busy absorbing the whole process here,
I tell you these people are only getting more
intense, the changes are slow, nothing has
happened drastically except for bizarre
butcher type murders at regular intervals.
I wonder about all I don't hear."*
**Letter from an American friend in Managua
November 26, 1979**

*"Our revolution is not a photograph to be
reproduced. It's an experience which has to
be studied, just as one studies the revolutionary
experiences of other peoples."*
—Tomas Borge, Comandante, FSLN, and Interior Minister, Government of National Reconstruction of Nicaragua

Five Views

"In December, cotton and coffee are harvested and we know we have to have a lot of cash on hand to pay the workers who had come from the south to harvest, but this December we did not plant, and we did not harvest, because we had no extra cash to buy fertilizers and irrigate and spray, and we just kept to ourselves up here, and it seemed unfair because the workers would be without, and they could afford it even less than us, but when January came around we were also very poor, and we sold the farm for half of what it was worth to an agent from the city. He was representing somebody big because he paid in cash, with American dollars, and we sold to him because the farm was all we had. But now what are we going to do? We have no way of buying another farm later, with so little money, and we are of the wrong class to hire out as day laborers. No Commuuists, if they should win in Nicaragua, would be worse to us than the people who boss us now ..."

A farmer's wife on the outskirts of Matagalpa in September 1978

"I joined the revolution because of the oppression. It was just very strong for many years in the north where I lived. My parents were farmers, but the oppression kept them poor. We had nothing and our lives were always being threatened even before the revolution. Is it any wonder that I grew up and decided to join a (clandestine) Sandinistan group, and when it was time I went into the mountains with the others. In the mountains we felt frightened but free. We knew we had to depend on each other, and also to be independent, free to take initiatives or suggest them to the others. It was an important time for all of us, but so was the oppression. I would not be here talking to you today, if we had not known about that."

"Gioconda," a Sandinistan woman soldier, September, 1979

"I can tell you it is a free country here and that makes me happy, but then you will say you are still hungry and poor, and we are. We are poorer than ever before, even under Somoza, but we are free to do something about our poverty now, if we choose. Nicaragua does not have to be this way. We all know that now from the revolution, whereas before it was known by only a very few, and they kept such secret information to themselves."

Manuel, a carpenter, in Leon.

"We made a lot of mistakes during the fighting, and we are still making mistakes. It's only natural because we are new to such liberties. We don't make bad mistakes. Maybe we will someday, but maybe we won't. We have to trust each other and believe we are good. The revolution taught us to have such hopes."

Victor, a Sandinistan *miliciano* in Diriamba, September, 1979.

MAXIMO

A college-educated agronomist, Maximo was a member of the moderate, Catholic Social-Democrat-oriented Tercerista faction of the Sandinistans, and he fought in Matagalpa before fleeing to Honduras. This interview was conducted in Mexico City in October 1979. He has visited the United States twice. In the late '60s he worked for a large American dairy company in Minnesota in a training program, and, in the middle '70s, lived for a while in Austin, Texas as a post-graduate student.

"We all thought we should fight. If we didn't fight the Marxists must take everything. So we fought and still they took a lot. I could go back to Nicaragua and I would be welcome because I have training. It's not that. I disagree. I never expected we would win every debate. We wished only to have a voice...I believe people of my training must lead, and if we are not believed, and they are preaching distrust, it's time to go. I miss my friends and the countryside. Some of my friends stayed. I don't grudge them that, and I have no use for counter-revolutionists. They wish only to bring back old Somoza, or his son...or friends...I have no use for that. People like my friends think they can trust the old business class. They'll turn around and have guns to their backs.

I was willing to die fighting with my friends. I am not willing to make war against old comrades. It would make me feel so foolish. To deny all is a bad thing. The people you will talk to in Nicaragua are hopeful, and those who are less hopeful are people from my class. Educated people... we know there are different ways... The rest see only that they have been given some kind of a chance, for their children, if not themselves.

If I had owned land, I would have stayed on and struggled. But I owned nothing except the skills I taught myself. Better to leave and sell the things I know about livestock to people who can pay me for my services.

It doesn't inspire me, but it means I am not turning against my own history.

The Somozas ruled so long and they never gave the people anything: not schools, nothing, in most places, in the countryside. We who tried a little could not succeed on our own so we went away. Now the people will try. They can't do any worse for themselves. Most of the time nobody even tried...

I will tell you this, finally: (in the old days) when you owned anything of value, one way or the other you bought it from the Somozas. So now there is a little less for people like me...It's only just, I suppose, because many should have guilty consciences. We all collaborated, and then we fought, but for us it was too late.

In the States you say of people when they die they "passed away." I think that is true of some of my class in Nicaragua. You will not be hearing from any of us again as Nicas. We are scattered: in New Orleans or San Francisco or San Jose, Costa Rica or here in the Federal District or in Pueblo or Monterrey. We all woke up much too late. When I go back someday I'll be just another tourist. If I like what I see I'll write a friend, and if I don't it's not my country any more.

You know, when we fought together in Matagalpa that first time there were many brave people. Some had only .22s or shot guns. The muchachos were fighting and dying and so were we, but it was different. They thought of dying without the same fear we had, who were closer to death in age...You can call that fanaticism, but I think it means they saw the future, and we were trying to barricade ourselves against the past...

So they died and we died, too, some of us. It was a struggle. An honorable man knows he must do certain things. If I wanted to be a killer all my life I would have joined old Somoza, and gotten rich, like all the rest, in Miami...

"Went to the fields beyond Tipitapa today to see how the cotton crop was, but no cotton crops were planted anywhere in that region because of the war. Those fields were now like small forests, and everybody in town seemed idle. A man told me nobody knew who owned the land around Tipitapa anymore or how to begin finding out."

From my September, 1979 diary.

*Those tropical nights of Central America were some-
times broken by the sounds of gunfire, even after the war
ended. Even then, the warm wet air yielded up a sharp
smell of cordite with sulphur, mingling the darker odors of
diesel exhaust and sewerage, spilled blood. Underneath its
broken buildings, Managua ripened old corpses; in jail
walls and garbage pits and dumps the broken bodies of
enemies of the former regime were still being found, and
at night, even now, there was a frequent din of guns firing,
new corpses, I assumed, were being made. The daily papers still displayed photos of those missing, presumed in
prison or dead. Everyday there were scores of such photos
from the old war. But that new corpses were being made
was denied whenever I asked the local security people
about it. Those shots, they told me, were caused by certain
edgy young Sandinistans on guard duty, or perhaps they
were celebrating, inappropriately, since the war had
ended some months back. But were there not still some of
Somoza's Guardsmen on the loose?*

*Yes, of course, indeed, they told me, and they have been
assassinating some of our people, so we have begun to
shoot to kill, if they will not be rounded up in peace,
because we are getting very angry at these counterrevolu-
tionaries, of the ultra left and the ultra right.*

"And those shots just now that sounded like volleys?"

"Just as I told you," said the local. "They were volleys."

"Not in front of this American journalist, compañero!"

*Our speaker had been interrupted by his superior, his
comandante, security person, handsome, of Chilean extraction. Clearly only so much free discussion was being
allowed in front of strangers like me about what was
going on. In the barrios, block by block and house by
house, at the closed meetings of the Sandinistan communes and committees of national defense (CDS), there
was much criticism and self-criticism allowed. But here,
in downtown Managua, in a hotel lobby, the nights often
seemed very very long and very dark.*

Once, leaving a junta press conference at the Casa del Gobierno at 7:30 in the evening, when it was already dark, I happened to be with the wife of an Interior Ministry official. (She was a journalistic colleague.) It was so dark we couldn't see twenty footsteps to either side of the well-lit and well-guarded government building where the conference had been held. We both felt a little frightened. Faced with so much darkness and ruined vacancy and the memory of so many shots at night, we drew ourselves back toward the light and then made excuses to each other: "I don't think I'm going to go home just right now..."

"Perhaps I'll stay with you..."

Luckily, just then, a taxi came along, going in a completely opposite direction. After hailing him down, we urged him to go our way and then drop off his fare. Or we would go along with him, wherever, just to get away from all that darkness.

As we drove away, my journalist friend told me in English, "It's really not a good idea to go anywhere in Managua at night right now. But if you go, you should go and then come back right away. Don't just be out on the streets. And don't just dawdle anywhere."

I was relieved to have such advice; whether it was from a colleague or a piece of Interior Ministry wisdom, did not, in fact, matter.

I remember, too, an anonymous poem I'd been reading in a collection of Nicaraguan revolutionary poems I'd bought at the university. It was called "Shots in the Night."

> *"Nobody knows anything,*
> *Some shots in the night have been heard.*
> *That's all..."*

One night, late, I heard real volleys, one every half hour or so, rifle fire, down the fill near the army base. They went on for some hours, like the sounds of executions. I went down into the hotel lobby to inquire what was happening. Nobody seemed to know. "It was just edgi-ness," said the chief of security.

The press did not report any executions ever. There were officially no executions. But there were revenge kil-lings. And what were they? Rifle fire, in volleys, late at night. What were they really? The old poem says "nobody knows why, or if they've been killed," and neither did I.

Once I asked a Mexican friend if he was ever scared in post-revolutionary Managua.

"Of course," he told me, "so I am rarely alone, if I can help it."

"Even when you're writing?"

"I write to defend the revolution," my friend told me, "not as any act of self-expression."

My Views

Early morning dawn during the rainy season in Managua came soft and blue; the air was always a little heavy and damp. From my hotel window, the ruined city I saw spreading below me looked somewhat more presentable than in direct sunlight, a city by a lake, like a miniature Chicago, it seemed; the long white sleek reach of the Bank of America's edifice climbed above the hulks of earthquake-broken buildings, empty lots, and hovels, all enveloped by this deep blue misty air.

In the early mornings there was bird song. The stink of so many diesels had not yet polluted the higher reaches of the city's many hills. And one could try to recuperate, then, from nights alone in a room, where the open windows shattered sleep even now, so long after the end of fighting, with all these sounds of gunfire: "... Shots by the cemetery wall ... "

Shortly after first dawn, I would go downstairs for coffee and a walk about the quiet streets. At that hour, the daily exhortations of the revolutionary left among this armed people had not yet begun. In some neighborhoods people got together before work to clean streets or stand in line for surplus commodities. They seemed calm and relieved at dawn after the terrors of certain Managua nights.

Some people I met talked fairly openly at such early hours. One morning I met a man from Masaya selling hammocks on a street corner to people passing by in their cars. They were ordinary white cotton hammocks, as he and his helpers had not yet been able to find any good dyes, but they were handsomely woven and intricate. I asked if he would still be at this place in one hour. If so, I would go back to my room and get money to purchase one for an American friend.

"Sorry I can't oblige you," he said, bowing. "Because it is really not likely. For I would attract too much attention being here that long, and besides," he told me, "a man like me has to be somewhat cautious as to how many hammocks he makes and how many he sells these days. It doesn't really pay to do too much business that people know about. So I'll keep my money in my pockets for a while longer," he told me, "because I wouldn't want to make myself too much business right now . . . until we see the way the wind blows . . ."

A Sandinistan policeman stood near by and said nothing to either of us. It was a normal street conversation in Managua after years of abnormal terror.

Despite edicts of the revolutionary government banning them, prostitutes still worked the outlying barrios of Managua during daytime as well as nighttime; and the pretty young boys who sometimes congregated at night around the Plaza España continued to perpetuate a professional underground of pederasty. Twice, when I stood amidst the nighttime traffic, after a rendezvous with an informant, I was propositioned by such avid, hungry, well-groomed youngsters: "Take me back to your hotel room meester!"

Managua was a place that by day seemed different from what it had been when fear and terror and corruption ruled, but by night seemed to revert just a little again. There were drugs for sale by the waiters in some of the better restaurants, if one wanted them, despite the pictures in *La Barricada* of marijuana crops being confiscated by young soldiers; and though police power was nowhere near as intrusive as I had remembered it being a year earlier, I couldn't help but recall a story I had heard from a reporter for *La Prensa* about one of Somoza's former police chiefs. When the U.S. Marines were sent in, after the earthquake of 1973, to keep the peace, they arrested this chief of police for dealing in drugs, and brought him to Somoza. "You can't do that," the Chief of State told them, and he sent his police chief abroad as one of his ambassadors until the marines left, and then recalled him to Nicaragua to be police chief again.

So Managua continued to be an evil city of every sort of commerce, even as ambitious plans were being readied to redevelop the earthquake-devastated downtown sections with parks and housing projects and stadiums; and despite so much new evidence of civic-mindedness emerging, there was a good deal of functional sleaziness left over from the earlier regime.

More and more the Nicaraguan state was what went on only in those sectors of the economy that had been expropriated from the Somozas and their followers, but it was hard, without "official guidance," to get access to such activities as the new "literacy schools" or the farm communes that had been given over to the peasantry. I was told it might take weeks to arrange, and I did not have the resources to wait around that long in Nicaragua.

But there was much to be seen. I revisited an old Creole friend in the Quinta Niña barrio and he told me he had been given work as a glorified file clerk in the Foreign Ministry because of his knowledge of English; he was very proud to have work because he had been a street boy before; and a young woman I knew had found work on the Sandinistan paper, *Barricada*. She said she was learning how to edit foreign news. When I told her I thought the paper was pretty crude and propagandistic, she did not disagree, but shrugged and said it would probably get better. "We are all beginners on *Barricada*," she told me. "But we had to start somehow."

Many of the men were still unemployed, but some were engaged in community activities, census taking, and clean-up work on a voluntary basis, and their families were being helped by U.S., Catholic, and other food-relief suppliers.

And, cautiously, like turtles peering out from their shells, the stores and restaurants and little factories were gradually coming back into business with a bare minimum of goods or inventories. They could always close up shop again and move elsewhere, to the States perhaps, if it didn't work out for them this time.

The Nicaraguan revolution was a revolution of the poor and the young and the Indians, and only later did the middle classes join in as a bridge, so it was not surprising that those who had become enfranchised and been given power by the revolution should be those who would be most enthusiastic in response to the changes that were taking place in Nicaraguan society. In nearly every encounter I had with authority, I was treated with a certain distance and distrust initially, but eventually with kindness and respect. Nobody seemed to wish to alienate anybody, if that could be avoided, but changes *were* taking place, and I—as a "transnational"—clearly might not sympathize.

A melancholy coffee farmer in Matagalpa showed me his family coffee tree (his "family tree" he called it) on the patio of his small half-ruined house and said, "This goes all the way back through the generations to when my family first came here, from Spain, but that's only one side of our story," he added, suddenly, lightening again, as if for my benefit. "The other side is we were always here, as Indians."

The government seemed to be trying to do all it could to encourage as many Nicaraguans as possible to feel a part of the new experience while, at the same time, it was rallying its strongest adherents in the barrios and countryside, and inciting them with revolutionary slogans, such as "repairing streets is also a revolutionary act" because it

knew the true desperation of the real bulk of its population, ill-housed, ill-clothed, ill-fed, with a 75-percent illi-
teracy rate, and very high infant-mortality rate.

The government seemed to know it needed time to
change all that, and it needed to have friends in the world
with resources, if it was to gain that time.

But at night in Managua it sometimes seemed that time
was very short. The sound of gunfire and the atmosphere
of terror seemed to suggest that forces were at work to
destroy all such good intentions.

The eight-year-old fair-haired, fair-skinned daughter of
the world famous star of rock 'n' roll, had high cheek
bones like her mother, who was much darker, and otherwise looked very much like her father, with whom she did
not live, there having been a divorce in the family; and
when her mother, of Nicaraguan birth, was conferring
with officials such as Tomas Borge, to help with "international solidarity," and raise medical and other emergency
funds, she stayed in the company of her middle-class
Nicaraguan grandparents and with an Indian nana who
spoke no English—logical, since she spoke no Spanish.

But whenever we met in the elevator of the hotel, this
pretty little girl of fastidious pronunciation always looked
wide-eyed and slightly harried, and she would glance over
her shoulders at that Indian woman of heavy bearing and
maternal manner, and demand to know did I speak Spanish, and if so could I please tell this woman not to follow
her about all the time?

There were armed soldiers everywhere and she was perfectly safe, the little girl averred, as I rapidly translated for
her, and then she added, "I'm simply trying to find my
mother in the lobby, don't you see?"

I saw, though the maid didn't always. She thought

loving someone meant keeping that someone close to your side. She followed the little girl everywhere, and they were sometimes accompanied by a dark-skinned boy the little girl's age, who was small and frail and good-looking, wore dark khaki military fatigues and also spoke no English.

He sometimes carried a wooden stick gun, as a toy, as did many Nicaraguan kids, and sometimes he would be all alone in the elevator when I came aboard, and I would pretend he had given me a very bad fright. "O... ¡hola! compañero," I would stumble, "tengo miedo (fear) de tal rifles... automáticos..."

He had a sad determined cast to his face, and I never got him to smile at my pranks in fumbling Spanish, and only once did I get him to speak at all. He said he would like a "duro," a coin, and I gave him a five-cordoba piece, and he expressed neither approval nor disapproval, just left me standing in the elevator going up, and went into the lobby, and we never spoke again.

The little rock 'n' roll heiress and her dark, quiet Nicaraguan companion (he was not to be considered a playmate) and the nana, were three of the least pretentious or ostentatious guests in the hotel.

There was the beautiful and showy blonde socialist journalist from Austria who pouted at every occasion she was greeted by American men, yet she wanted to be greeted, that was clear, for she dressed in stylish see-through skirts and blouses, her breasts prominent and her legs stockinged. Her husband was working on a project in the jungle and the only time I can remember her being pleasant to anybody, except a top-ranking Sandinistan, was one morning over breakfast when I demanded to know if her dress, high-heeled shoes, and sheer stockings were intended for her forthcoming visit to her husband in the jungle. She blushed and confessed she simply could not find a pair of boots to fit her.

There was a balding fat gnome of an American journalist in the hotel, the only other U.S. journalist I encountered this time, and he was full of hate for everybody: Russians, Nicaraguans, fellow journalists, and especially World-Bank Germans whom he accused of every Nazi crime, though some were born as late as 1946.

There were currency speculators (still legal), international civil servants (low-key), the new Indian ambassadress (in a blue sari and dark blue hair to match), and a number of hustlers and U.S. businessmen.

Quite the most interesting and bizarre of these was the fair-haired brutish man I shall call Gus, from California, who was just in the process of making a large deal to ship relief supplies for the entire revolutionary junta.

Making large deals was nothing new to Gus, a former truck driver, who claimed he was a multimillionaire in the trucking, warehousing, and shipping business. This was only his first trip abroad, and he was truly shocked by what he'd seen of Nicaragua.

"I never realized it was so bad for people down here," he kept telling us, in the bar, "so many people hungry and homeless, so many poor and wounded, and so many deaths..."

He told me he was a conservative at home, but even so he just couldn't believe people were as mean and stingy as the Somozas had been.

"Why not give the people something?" He claimed to have told the junta as part of his sales pitch. "If you make ten million that's OK, but make sure the people get a million too. It's only fair. In my place, I only employ Chicanos, and some of them don't even have their green cards, but believe me I pay what I have to pay—top dollars..."

I wondered what the Marxist members of the junta, with whom he'd been meeting privately to clinch the deal, would have thought of such a nineteenth-century "liberal" capitalist. Gus was so tactless and frank I came to enjoy his capsule descriptions of the junta members with whom he'd met.

Of Comandante Daniel Ortega Saavedra, for example,

he told me "that's one very tough son of a bitch . . . Oooo I mean it," he exclaimed.

Interior Minister Tomas Borge was also likened to "a little bull of a guy. I mean he's business."

But, despite his crudities, Gus was obviously impressed with the seriousness of junta members and their reconstruction efforts. He said he could save them about $6000 on every containerized shipment of relief supplies over a competing Japanese firm, and he'd throw in extras, for no cost, or at wholesale: free warehousing and inventory record-keeping, even, if necessary, a whole division's worth of U.S. arms (M-16s) and equipment. I sometimes wondered whether Gus had a silent partner in Langley, Virginia he wasn't telling me about, and if all the naivete was just show.

He wouldn't let me pay for a single drink at the bar, nor, for that matter, would he let anybody else, and he even treated some of the regulars to evenings at a nearby brothel, had found himself a local girl and a particular outdoor taco stand he liked, and declared he thought Nicaraguan government beef was great, and he was hoping to do business with the revolution—communist or no.

An impressive combination of cliché and candor, brute bigotries and open-mindedness, he hated blacks but claimed to love Chicanos, and wasn't too fond of Israelis either, it seemed, which may have put him in very good shape with the junta.

He didn't like it if you left him at the bar alone, and since he knew he wasn't supposed to wander around Managua at night, Gus could be very persuasive about keeping the bar open, and drinks going around, and "Oh stay and have another," and all kinds of shit like that.

And to think that people like Gus were probably of more immediate use to the new government of Nicaragua, than the young poet protégé of Ernesto Cardenal's I met, whom nobody at the Ministry of Culture had the time to speak to because—though he'd translated the great *Zero Hour* and gotten it wide attention here—he was, after all, an American, and subtle in his approach, or shall we say crafty.

"If you tell anybody about how rotten I'm feeling," he confided to me once, "I'll haunt you. I'll kill you."

I don't know what he had to say to Gus, with whom he also drank a lot: a combination of wind and rain, oil and water, or even fire and ice.

In the foyer of El Retiro, bare now except for some colorful revolutionary posters on the wall, the housewife from Managua straightened her dark shingle-cut hair before a mirror and patted her small, dark, frowning eleven-year-old daughter on the shoulder: "So this is where the great man was living. So? I see ... "

"This was Somoza's wife's house," I corrected her.

"Indeed?" She seemed puzzled, quizzical. "Do you mean Doña Hope or the other woman?"

"Doña Hope," I said, "the wife. It was a family house ... "

"Indeed," she muttered again, "indeed. His wife," and she patted her little girl again, and drew her close to her.

From a patio came squeals of flute practice. El Retiro is now the Ministry of Culture, and its ground floors and gardens are given over almost entirely to young students of the arts: dancers, musicians, theatre people. Above are the offices of poet-priest Ernesto Cardenal, Minister of Culture, and his numerous well-bred female assistants.

The house itself has lost most of its lush accoutrements and looks a little like a large expensive tract home in Great Neck. To get there one drives half a mile or more through the former properties of the Somoza and Portacarrera families, adjacent to the posh mall called the Plaza De España.

The woman had opened a closet door and found it

empty, except for some reams of typewriter paper. I followed her and her daughter toward the step-down living room and she gasped, "How lovely," when she saw the entire wall of tinted dark glass facing out onto the former gardens.

There were plants in grotesque clay pots with ears, and a young girl was sitting with a large drawing pad and making a sketch of a flamboyant tree.

The woman saw me following her and blushed and said, "I remember Doña Hope. How could we forget her? She was such a well-brought-up lady..."

"I have heard that," I said.

"A true Doña," she said, "but Tacho he liked Dinora better because she was so vulgar."

"Do you think that's why?"

"It's true," she said, "and if my daughter were not with me here I would tell you certain things about that man..."

"Such as?"

"It's better that I not say more," she said. "I brought my daughter here because I want to encourage her to study music." Darkening, she pushed her daughter ahead of her into the next room.

I followed her there and could hear her explaining to the little girl, like a tourist guide, how Doña Hope was a true lady but Dinora was certainly a *puta*, a whore, and Somoza made her brother a colonel in the army just to have this mulatta.

She said, "He was an awful man, Tacho. He used to say he could not stand Doña Hope's voice because it was so frail and refined."

"Did you know him personally?" I asked.

"We all knew him," she said. "He was the boss."

"Did you know him personally?" I inquired again.

"For a little while my husband was a family chauffeur." She stared down at the worn gold cotton carpeting. "That is a long time ago meester. My daughter never knew. She's a good girl," she told me. "Talented and bright..."

"And where is your husband now?"

"In the States," she said. "He won't be coming back to Nicaragua."

She drew the little girl close to her again and walked on into the next room.

As I left El Retiro that day the woman and her daughter seemed to be following me. I heard her explaining to the child that the big man had lived here in all this splendor with his wife Doña Hope and their children, but he, like so many others, would never be coming back to Nicaragua in her lifetime, and it was necessary to make the most of the changes taking place which could lead to opportunities for people like them, now that there were even some women in the government which had not been the case in Tacho's day.

They were walking down the roadway ahead of me, arm in arm, with a forlorn grace, and when I drove past—some few minutes later—they were already quite a way down the road in the twilight, but were pleased now to accept a ride to the bus station where they could find transportation back to their house in the Tiscapa barrio of Managua.

On the first day of registration at the National University in Managua the day's events included an address by the director of the Sandinistan Youth Movement and a baseball game. There were book peddlars hawking paperback translations of Camus and Marx and Gramsci; American culture was represented by a number of editions of the works of Irving Wallace.

The university had been pretty much closed down over the last couple of years, and its walls were still daubed with large anti-Somoza murals and slogans. It was here, within one of these classrooms, that I had met briefly with student representatives of the Marxist MPU in the middle of the war, and they had patiently answered every question

I could ask about their activities in organizing the barrios. Some students had been murdered on these grounds by National Guard paramilitaries in years past, but now young men and women waited on line patiently, in casual clothes, to enroll in classes, and there was a good deal of easy flirtation and chit chat.

A young man told me, "I was the first in my family to get an education, and then for two years that education was denied us, as a punishment, in part. We all feel behind the times, but we're hopeful now."

The young woman on the road out of Tipitapa was going to "borrow" milk for her family from a cousin who had a farm ten miles farther down the road. She carried it back along the highway in a two-gallon pail, the milk slopping a little over the sides. She told me it would be used for making a milky cheese, a Nicaraguan staple, into which tortillas are sometimes dipped.

Struggling with her heavy burden, she gladly accepted when I offered her a lift home.

She told me today was the first day of school for her, and since she no longer had to work in the cotton fields this time of year, she was celebrating by doing an extra chore for her hard-pressed family.

Diriamba was still a city under arms, and in the town's only cinema a great many young Sandinistan soldiers with time on their hands were being shown Cuban movies.

In the turmoil and noisy darkness of the cinema the

movies reminded me of some of the U.S. Army training films shown to us in Fort Chaffee, Arkansas, in the late 1950s. Then the enemy was world communism; now he was Tío Sam, Imperialism, and Oligarchy. True enough, I suppose, but the films were really rather crude, and boring, except for some very funny cartoons in which *campesinos* outsmarted Tío Sam and the *latifundistas* in true Tom-and-Jerry style.

But the feature, in scratchy black and white, was a history of the Cuban Revolution. The sound track was unclear, but the messages came through: in less than three minutes we saw miserable Cuban sugar workers kneeling before the whip of the crooked plantation owners; they seemed poor and miserable and sickly, unable even to organize demonstrations to protest their rights before the appearance of the terrible police on horseback.

Then we cut to the prow of Castro's ship *Granma* cutting through the Caribbean, and we saw actors dressed as Castro and Camillo and the others in fatigues in a forest grove, shaking hands with all the workers solemnly, and offering them pistols with which to revolt. A moment or two later Castro was entering Havana in triumph, and the U.S. gangsters were fleeing, with all the *gusanos*, and, on a nearby U.S. aircraft carrier, planes were being readied for an air strike.

Well I guess as history goes this isn't so wrong: it's just trimmed down quite a bit, so as to be dull and meaningless.

The young Sandinistan *milicianos* seemed rather restless and a little bored; they whistled and made catcalls to one another as I went back out into the light of day.

An armed young *miliciano* was standing by the door waiting to get inside.

"What kind of movies do we have today?" he asked.

"A Cuban film," I told him, "the history of Castro and the *gringos*."

"That again," he said. "I've seen it."

"Are there no others?" I asked.

"For us there is just no money," he said, "and therefore we have to see the same movies over and over again, and there is nothing much else to do...at present..."

"That doesn't sound very nice," I said.

"It could be better," he told me, "but also it could be worse. None of our leaders speak to us for four hours at a time, like Castro, but perhaps someday they will..."

"Do you believe so?"

"Who knows meester?" He pushed past me inside to the darkness.

Leaving

On my last Sunday in Nicaragua I took a cab out of Managua to the country. The driver had other passengers. He would take me to Masaya, but first he had to drop them off in a place called Caterina, which is about five kilometers from the back entrance into Monimbo.

It was a beautiful dark-green and bright morning, after a heavy downpour, and the fields everywhere were sprouting corn and hay and alfalfa. Nowhere I had ever been seemed as lush and fertile as that countryside; it seemed barely depleted after all those years of bloodletting.

Most of the movable wreckage of warfare had been carted away, and the battered little towns we passed that bright lovely Sunday were bedecked with thousands of *rojonegro* Sandinistan pennants, in front of every doorway, strung between the streets six and seven times across, at every corner. The countryside was at such peace; people were beginning to visit their relatives once more.

In the cab with me were a pharmacist from Managua and a young *miliciano*; the cab was a battered old Datsun, and the driver had turned off his meter to charge us all the flat rate, fifty cordobas a piece for the forty-kilometer trip. He was a gentle man, and he sang and played his radio to accompany his singing as we traveled. Meanwhile my

two companions talked to each other about baseball in a
very slangy Spanish so that I could only make out every
two or three words they said, and I was saying very little
myself, listening all the while, and hoping to improve my
Spanish comprehension.

There's a little village before you reach Caterina where
an anti-tank ditch had been dug by Sandinistans to defend
the *entrada*. It was only about a foot and a half wide, but
maybe ten feet deep and a hundred yards across, and it had
collected a good deal of trash.

In order to enter this village, where the militiaman
wished to be dropped, our Datsun had to make its way
across that ditch, but halfway over its wheels began to
spin; we smelled burning rubber and were stuck there
right in the middle.

"How awful," our cabby declared, and he pushed open
the door and jumped out, his three other passengers following him. The car began to tilt crazily to one side, over
the ditch.

At that moment a young militiaman appeared wearing
a fatigue cap with a gold star and, slung across his
shoulder, an M-16. He was also wearing an expensive raw
silk sports jacket, liberated from a Somocista household,
or so it seemed, and blue jeans; from inside his sports coat
he removed a pencil and a small pad and began to scribble
a note.

We were getting a ticket, on a piece of paper from a pad
with a Bayer aspirin logo, for getting stuck in that ditch.

In Somoza's time, I thought, the National Guard held
you up for a lot of money; now they gave you tickets. But
my cabby was highly incensed. With hands on his hips he
glanced toward his car and then back again at the armed
miliciano, breathing hard, as he silently cursed at all his
bad luck.

"Shit man..."

The militiaman handed him that Bayer aspirin paper
and started to wag his finger: "You might have destroyed
this vehicle. Now is not the time for that. Reckless driving.

Transportation is a vital resource of the revolution."

"*Ojalá*," was all the cabby could say: "I hope so..."

But his other *miliciano* passenger, who had caused his problem to begin with, said much more. He was a thin young sharp-faced boy of fifteen with alert brown eyes. Noticing all the townspeople gathered about the ditch, he declared, "Well who will help this good man with a push?"

"*Vamanos cumpas*," he added.

People were not too sure whether to help or not, since the cabby had just been handed a ticket, and the Sandinistan *miliciano*, armed, was still standing about. He was so young and callous looking, and he had his weapon trained on us.

"Let's go," he urged, a second time, and when he put his shoulder to the window of the driver's side I went and pushed from the rear. Then the pharmacist from Managua, and the policeman in the sports jacket, his liberated rifle banging in its sling against the trunk when he leaned over to push, and the two young peddler women from the town, and a couple of the little boys also joined in.

The cabby leaped behind the wheel and turned on his ignition and with a heave and a shove we lifted the front end of the car out of the ditch and pushed it back onto the road where it could turn about again under its own power.

All three passengers got aboard, and the driver thanked those who had helped, even the policeman who had given him the ticket. The policeman now waved his pad in the air and cautioned him, "You must remember it is official, even though I do not yet have the proper forms."

"Agreed," the driver said. But as we started down the muddy street to drop off our young passenger as close to his house as that anti-tank ditch would allow, I asked, "What is one supposed to do with such a ticket?"

"Who knows?" the cabby shrugged. "Nobody knows. It is a mystery of the revolution."

And all three Nicaraguans in the car began to chuckle softly to themselves.

The young militiaman paid with an American dollar and that was accepted for the equivalent of forty cordobas.

As we drove away the cabby said, "Papers and words they never meant justice here in Nicaragua," and he crumpled up his summons, and threw it into the revolutionary anti-tank ditch.

Then the pharmacist made a joke: "Would you like a safe conduct scribbled on a prescription for nembutals?"

"Who needs sleeping pills?" said the cabby. "This place is putting me to sleep."

We were near Caterina now, and not too far away was another ditch where many young boys and girls from Monimbo had been herded together during the revolution by Somoza's National Guard and executed.

Now the fields were lush and green; cattle lowed; a cornfield was thickly sprouting afresh.

I asked to be dropped off; I'd walk in to Masaya through the back entrance of Monimbo.

As I paid the driver, he thanked me for helping with his car.

Then he said I must not assume he was against the revolution. He just did not like this new bureaucracy any better than the old, well maybe just a little, but they were still such "amateurs," and he did not like the Cubans.

The pharmacist said "When we all fought it was different. People behaved better."

"Everybody behaved well then," the cabby put in, "because they had to. Nicaragua should be proud of that time."

"Exactly," the pharmacist said.

"*Vaya bien*," I said.

"You go well," they told me and drove off together.

Notebook entry, February 1980:

Marco wants me to help him write the history of the Somoza dynasty going back to the nineteenth century and the first of the Somozas, who was a highwayman in the era shortly after Walker and the Filibusters invaded Nicaragua.

He wants to write about the Vanderbilts, how they made their fortune in Nicaragua, and about Somoza, who was a used-car salesman in Salt Lake City and learned English there, and about Somoza, the lavatory attendant, and FDR and Somoza ("He's our son-of-a-bitch."). This whole history of Somocism in Central and South America would, in effect, be a history of U.S.-Latin American relations over more than a century. His working title is "The Satrap," as in the times of the Turkish empire.

I endeavor to act as his agent here. Nobody is interested. Publishers say it's all over down there. Who cares? We're not interested anymore. Americans are not interested in books on Central America. They don't sell. Nobody, except for one publisher, is even interested in seeing the prospectus.

The work may require a number of years time, so I advise Marco, who is also not a rich man, I must abandon working with him on it. He should endeavor to sell it in Spain, where he is, at least, known as a fine, published author.

He writes back "maybe it's because it's so close they just don't care the Yankees... or because they lost." Maybe, I have to admit, or maybe it's just a matter of dollars and cents. When I was in Central America, Iran and Nicaragua were both in turmoil.

The correspondent for Time *complained to me that his cover story on Somoza's atrocities had just been bumped for an account of Iranian atrocities.*

He said, "It's not surprising, I suppose. We own a bunch of television stations and radio stations in Iran. We don't own anything here that I know of."

Dear Marco:

With regret I write to say I cannot be of help to you on your project. I wish I knew how to help you write a best-seller such as Chesapeake *about the Somoza dynasty. From what I can figure out, I don't believe any American publisher would be interested, and I don't know how to write bestsellers myself. Maybe we should be writing poems and stories of intensity and candor. Isn't that what some aspects of the revolution were about? For men to be honest again...*

I embrace you

Richard

Translation of a letter received from Marco.
October 12, 1980:

Dear Good Friend:

...I must beg your pardon that I have not been able to write you before this. Your correspondence helps my good health considerably; good health composed more of lead than steel, the health of a poet who prefers his own country to exile. If I have not been able to write before this, you should understand it has been as much because of my business as my lugubrious mood.

The death of Somoza (assassinated in Paraguay) made me smile. Now he can't be hated. It was a bitter smile, though, in that I realized that the supposed "sons of Sandino" have become, in actuality, sons of Somoza by learning from the late-defunct National Guard the same militaristic ideas. All sons-of-bitches are alike (repeated in English in parentheses).

I have so many things to recount to you. Today I have received a letter with ten Swiss francs from you for books. Alas, these are no longer exchangeable on the black market...Sometime soon I hope to be able to turn, once again, to making poems.

I don't happen to believe in anything anymore except the fearsome God of the Old Testament. Your poems kept me awake all one night. I shall try to reproduce some in our press in translation. The dedication to me compromised my heart where it felt touched.

M.